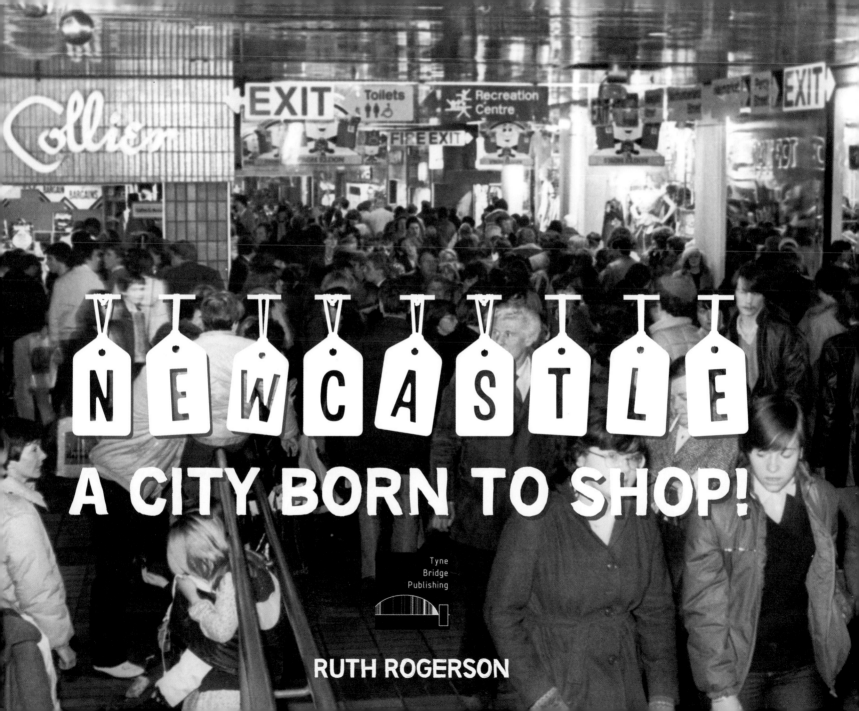

NEWCASTLE
A CITY BORN TO SHOP!

Tyne
Bridge
Publishing

RUTH ROGERSON

First published in the UK in 2018 by

Tyne Bridge Publishing, City Library,
Newcastle upon Tyne, United Kingdom
tynebridgepublishing.org.uk

ISBN-13: 9780951048856

Photographs and images from Newcastle Libraries Archives unless
otherwise stated.

Image research by Shawn Fairless
Edited by Vanessa Histon
Design by David Hepworth

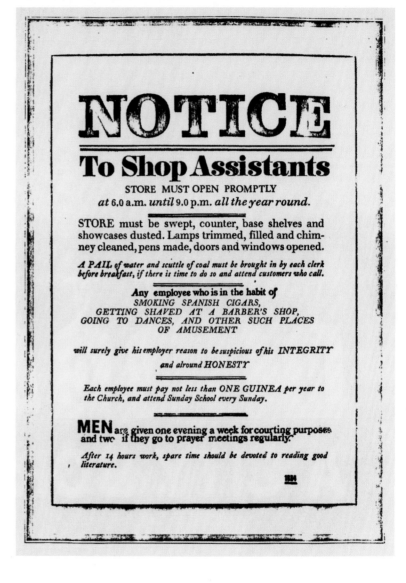

ABOVE) A NOTICE FOR EMPLOYEES – NO FLEXI TIME, NO MATERNITY LEAVE, NO PAID LEAVE, NO ERR... SPANISH CIGARS.
NEXT PAGE, CLOCKWISE FROM TOP LEFT. 1) A BUSY NORTHUMBERLAND STREET, 1956. 2) FREEMAN'S ON THE JUNCTION
OF PUDDING CHARE AND BIGG MARKET, DECIMAL PRICES ON DISPLAY IN 1971. 3) A CARTOON FROM 1907 BEMOANING THE
NUMBER OF ADVERTS AND 'SKY SIGNS' IN NEWCASTLE.

The above sketch is intended to give some slight idea of what one of Newcastle's principal thoroughfares will be like ff the increase of sky signs and scare advertisements continues.

THE BIGG MARKET, 1928

INTRODUCTION

The Haymarket; Bigg Market; Cloth Market; Groat Market; Market Street. Have you ever thought about how many place names in Newcastle refer to shopping? We sometimes talk about places in passing without giving any real thought to how their names came to pass, and that is without even considering the modern day mecca of Eldon Square, the timelessly fascinating Grainger Market, the sweeping beauty of Central Arcade or the street synonymous with shopping, Newcastle's very own version of London's Oxford Street: Northumberland Street. Newcastle is a city built on its market history, it is a city born to shop!

Even before King John made Newcastle upon Tyne a borough in 1216, traders had already set up stall in markets along Great North Road, which linked to the old Tyne Bridge, a shopping location in itself, and provided the town's main thoroughfare. In a similar way to motorway service stations today, passing trade provided a captive audience and market traders were the Alan Sugars of their time, spotting business opportunities and capitalising on them.

Newcastle's riverside location also provided ample opportunity for trade. The Quayside area was the perfect spot for setting up stall in addition to shop-keeping ventures where wealthy merchants lived in grand homes above pokey shops that belied their fortunes. We're fortunate that T Dan Smith's 1960s' concrete utopia that decimated much of upper Newcastle didn't stretch down to the banks of the Tyne, meaning many of the old 'shops' are still around today, though they have taken up different residents. Many now house bars and restaurants rather than their traditional wares: the familiar sight of the Cooperage, built in the 15th century, was a barrel-makers in its heyday, now if you can find any barrels on the premises they might house only kegs of beer as its last incarnation was as a pub.

As the dene on creatively titled, Dean Street, was filled in at the end of the eighteenth century, the physical barrier between the upper and lower town was removed and allowed trade to expand throughout the nineteenth century. We may well curse that steep hill now when trying to walk up it, particularly in heels, but we should be thankful it is there: its creation heralded the foundations of the shopping scenes we recognise today.

But what of the names of the marketplaces around town, what do they actually mean? Did the Bigg Market just sell large items? There was a whole market for Groats…but what the heck is a Groat? Answers do not need to be sent on a postcard as can be found henceforth!

Although we now consider any form of purchase as 'shopping', in years gone by there was a distinction between 'shopping' and 'marketing': by which I do not mean the fancy promotion of goods or services to entice us to favour one brand over another, which 'marketing' refers to these days. In Victorian times shopping was a leisurely pursuit which ladies undertook to meet their friends in town, whereas marketing involved buying everyday goods and was something the servant classes or poor folk did; what market they frequented depended on their fresh food needs of the day…

NEWCASTLE'S OLD MARKETS

SANDHILL MARKET

'Ye olde ancient' Sandhill Market was found at the foot of the Side at Cale Cross; now an unsightly, as most are, office block. Proximity to the Quayside and bridge over the Tyne made it a popular market choice where traders sold eggs, milk, butter and poultry. Fairness was the order of the day and in 1724 a Cooper, G Henderson, was appointed as a 'prototype' Market Inspector, his role was to ensure quality and quantity of goods. Nine years later, the market was gripped in scandal - 1733 was the year Miles Hogg was stripped of twenty firkins of butter as they were underweight; a crime Mr Lurpak would never dare commit these days. Sandhill also had a herb market and fish market, which moved to Newgate Street in 1898, however, possibly due to the butter outrage, it remained best known for its dairy produce.

Gradually, as the upper town developed the upper echelons of society moved with it, leaving the Quayside and its markets to the poorer folk in toon. Markets are supply and demand mechanisms and as such demand for cheaper goods meant a change in produce; the Monday Market became a last chance saloon for the meat that wasn't snapped up the previous Saturday at the upper towns Flesh Market and a second hand clothes market on Saturday meant the financially deprived didn't have to run around in the nuddy. Rumours that this market did not sell coats, perhaps the origin of the well-known fact that Geordies won't wear coats even in the coldest weather, cannot be confirmed. The Sunday morning Quayside Market stretched from Sandhill to Sandgate and is still a popular haunt for shoppers today, though the traders of 1736 would probably be bemused by the 'artisan' title of produce today, which they would consider their basic groceries.

SANDHILL WITH NEWCASTLE'S GUILDHALL

BIGG MARKET

Though the Bigg Market of modern times may often be referred to as a 'meat market', albeit for a wholly different reason, it has never been a market place for meat. Similarly though it was indeed once very big, stretching from Nun Street to Pudding Chare where it divided into three: the Groat Market to the west, Middle Steet, and Cloth Market to the east; the Bigg title actually derives from its produce: barley. Way back in 1388 it was known as a 'beremarket', which can be translated to a barley market in modern day English and the name 'Bigg' refers to a variety of barley which had four rows of grain on each ear. So now you know.

Its reputation for revelry may not be an entirely modern mischief. In 1879 local businesses complained of the interruptions caused by the market, leading to a bylaw in 1884 which attempted to control the running of the market: though many may argue the Bigg Market has always been and always will be, the place to be out of control.

GROAT MARKET

We have become fond in recent times of merging words together to create one; examples being 'hangry' whereby you are so hungry you are angry, or couple names such as 'Brangelina' for the now separated and therefore singular again 'Brad and Angelina' however this is not a new concept and the Groat Market is an example. What name would you give to grains of oats? Groats of course! What name would you therefore give to a market that sold Groats? It's a difficult one so I'll leave that one with you…

THE BIGG MARKET IN MORE PASTORAL TIMES.

ABOVE) A VERY EARLY IMAGE OF THE GROAT MARKET

CLOTH MARKET

The origin of this market's name is interesting given that it is an area now classed by many as simply part of the Bigg Market. The Cloth Market was formerly known as the Flesh Market and therefore sold meat. Whether flesh will one day be covered by cloth in the Bigg Market on a Friday or Saturday night however remains to be seen.

'Ye olde' Friday nights in this part of town saw butchers erecting their stalls ready for Saturday morning trading; stalls known as 'shambles' from the Saxon word 'scamel', a bench where butchers cut their meat: so perhaps this section of town now classed as the Bigg Market is indeed rightly referred to as the 'meat market' after all!

The naming of the Cloth Market relates to fairs on Lammas Day (1st August) and St Lukes day (18th October) where drapers and blanket dealers flocked to the area to sell their wares, which they did until 1885. This market was another which attracted fraudsters, so much so that a 'pillory' or stocks were placed in the market in an attempt to detract cheats. Crime however has no deterrant for some and in 1836 John 'Tricky' Hall was placed in the pillory for rubbing out the receipt of a bond; he remained there for two hours from noon to 2pm to enable others to pelt him with rubbish for his sins.

HAYMARKET

No prizes for guessing the produce this market sold…

If I asked you to name one of the perks of being a Freeman of the City of Newcastle I'm sure you would say 'being able to graze your cows on the Town Moor'. Indeed this

PADDY'S CLOTHES MARKET IN SANDGATE - RALPH HEDLEY

may well be the only perk as no one seems to know what being a Freeman of Newcastle actually means, other than you can park your cows on the Town Moor. If you have cows, you need to feed them. If you have cows on the Town Moor it would therefore be handy to have a market nearby where you could purchase fodder and other cow related goods, hence in 1824 the Haymarket was established for all your farming needs. If you are a weary farmer having to trudge into town for your cattle feed, it's likely you will need somewhere to rest and some entrepreneurial brightspark built a pub and hotel on that very spot; the latest version of The Farmer's Rest built in 1920, was knocked down in 1995 to make way for the new bus station and Marks and Spencer.

HAYMARKET, 1959.

GREEN MARKET

This market was a bit of a nomad around Newcastle for 400 years until the big bad City Council finally killed it off in 2011. Alas it wasn't a market where you could only buy green things, a full rainbow spectrum of coloured items could actually be found; the origin of the name 'Green' Market is however open to debate.

It started off as a street market opposite St Andrew's Church near Newgate Street before taking up residency in a section of the 1808 butchers' market called 'Green Court', this may be where it got its name from, rather than as many people assume, due to it selling fruit and vegetables. This building was demolished when Richard Grainger started redeveloping the city in the 1830s and the market then set up stall in large sheds in Clayton Street opposite the Grainger Market, before hotfooting it over to Eldon Square in 1976. It remained resident here until 2007 when again its home was pulled down, this time for the modernisation of Eldon Square. The Council said the market could move instead to High Friars on a temporary basis until a permanent space could be found, however the permanent space turned out to be the confines of history as it was later decided that the market had no home in the revamped shopping mall and was no longer economically viable. Unlike the other market places and perhaps because it always was a market on the move, there is now no part of Newcastle known as the 'Green Market', which is a shame given the lengthy existence it once had.

I remember the Bigg Market and Green Market when there were ladies selling seafood from old prams. I used to love to go there with my mother to buy crabs. Later in my years I went with friends and enjoyed snacks at Milburn's Oyster Bar whilst the men went off to Robinson's Wine Cellar for a pint of Mackeson.

Kathleen Jan

The Green Market was always a treat with my gran when I was a kid, the 'weigh-in' sweet shop was a must visit!

Caroline McLaughlin

Sarah Gaskin's flower shop in the Green Market was always on our list of places to visit as my gran used to work there. The lovely smell of all the fresh flowers made it a market favourite.

Pat Rogerson

The Green Market was opposite the Co-op Stores and had two rows of stalls. It was always very noisy as the stallholders called out their wares to attract customers. Some stalls were always busy with (not always orderly!) queues or groups of customers trying to get served. I felt it was a shame when it got demolished and the stalls were moved into the Grainger Market.

Anne Nelson

I remember the old greenmarket, that was somewhere to go with Dad to buy the odd dahlia and other garden plants. Locally grown, they didn't come in pots but in big trays of earth. A small trowel was used to get them out then they were wrapped in newspaper.

Sue Holdroyd

NEXT PAGE, CLOCKWISE FROM TOP LEFT. 1) SELLING FRUIT AND VEGETABLES, 1970. 2) PIGEONS FOR SALE. 3) THE FAMOUS ESCALATORS, 1982. 4) 1970.

THE NORTH END OF NORTHUMBERLAND STREET IN THE EARLY 1980S. OF COURSE FENWICKS AND MARKS & SPENCER REMAIN, BUT EVERYTHING ON THE RIGHT HAND SIDE HAS CHANGED. C&A IS NOW PRIMARK. THE CALLERS BUILDING HAS BEEN HAMLEYS, HMV AND IS NOW JD SPORTS.

UNDERCOVER SHOPPING

A natural progression from open air market trading was to create undercover outlets so that shoppers could hide from the north east chill and shop i
peace from pesky rain. In time, such centres even became shopping hubs in themselves, go-to venues for shoppers in need of a retail therapy to enhanc
their purchasing pleasure!

Off the top of your head name a shopping mall in Newcastle…let me guess, you said Eldon Square right? As the big daddy of undercover shopping i
Newcastle it's not surprising if it's the venue that first springs to mind, yet it isn't the only weather friendly shopping location in Newcastle and give
how malls have come and gone, chances are it won't be the last: remember the Royal Arcade? Handyside Arcade? Leazes Arcade? No? Well here's
reminder of Newcastle's shopping venues past and present…

GRAINGER MARKET

In the 1830s, a certain Richard Grainger was at play, designing much of the Newcastle we see today and what many would regard as the best bits o
architecture in the city. Grey Street being regularly voted best street in Britain is proof of this, but we don't need proof as us Geordies know it's tru
anyway. Grainger's vision involved dividing the Bigg Market from Grainger Street and demolishing the Butchers' market, which was previously nea
High Bridge Street. To keep the displaced butchers happy, he built a new home for them, funding half of the £36,000 needed to build the marke
himself, which showed his confidence in his plans. At the time, this venture became the largest covered market in Europe and in 1835 the Grainge
Market was born, becoming a precursor to late night shopping with opening hours from 6am to 10pm and staying open all night on Fridays…whic
would surely be welcomed by late night revellers today.

> I remember going to the Grainger Market, it was the late 80s and Thatcher was still on the 'throne'. I was on a
> full student grant of £1,300 a year. Money was tight so I used to stake out all the bargains, being careful to
> make sure they gave me the fruit and veg from the front that wasn't bruised!
>
> *J Dibdon*

> As a child growing up in the 50s and 60s my memories of shopping in Newcastle include a few places that I
> visited on a regular basis. We visited the Grainger Market fairly often and I loved it. An exotic place filled with
> colour, noise, a variety of smells, some more pleasant than others, and, most memorably, men in white coats
> dashing through the market aisles carrying whole dead pigs over their shoulders. To a small child, this sight
> was both fascinating and frightening in equal measure.
>
> *Kath Cassidy*

FROM TOP LEFT. 1) ENTRANCE TO MARKET FROM NUN STREET. 2) BARGAIN HUNTING AT THE ORIGINAL PENNY BAZAAR. 3) SPOT SID JAMES ADVERTISING FRUIT, 1970. 4) A BANQUET GIVEN IN HONOUR OF GRAINGER AT THE OPENING OF THE MARKET PAINTED BY HENRY PERLEE PARKER IN 1835 (TWAM).

The Grainger Market always was and still is a favourite place of mine to simply walk around, marvel at the goods on offer and take in the atmosphere of a bustling market. There was the usual banter coupled with a very high standard of product knowledge as there were so many specialised sellers.

Simon Carey

I always liked the Grainger Market, my mother used to as well. We used to find bargains in fruit, veg and meat. I didn't like it in the 60s when they used to hang rabbits and hares upside down in butchers' shops with a cup over the head to catch the drips of blood. The butchers sold other game meat in the same way.

Madeleine Lydia Duployen

In the 60s, my parents asked me to go to Oliver & Eden's in the Grainger Market each week to get a sheep's head for my Alsatian dog, Bryn. One day I went to the chiropodists in the Bigg Market after collecting the head. After the chiropodist had finished with my feet I then took the trolley bus home to the West End of Newcastle. A couple of hours later, a very agitated chiropodist rang me to ask if my feet were all right. Apparently, as he left the surgery he had found a trail of blood in the waiting room. I quickly reassured him that as I mounted the bus, I had noticed that the sheep's head which was wrapped in brown paper, had been leaking blood. Danger averted!

Linda Gallagher

Napoleon described the British as a nation of shop keepers. Maybe he should have said a nation of shoppers. My earliest memories are of the meat market which I visited regularly as a child. My father worked for years in a butchers, thus being nicknamed 'Bob the Butcher' by family and friends. The shop, which is still there, was narrow with a long frontage and tiny office in one corner. The office was about the size of two telephone kiosks side by side. It had glass all round so whoever was inside could see the shop clearly to keep an eye on things.

I loved being there perched on a high stool at the desk, which was built in across the narrow end of the office. The phone, the candlestick type, was a real novelty as I knew no one posh enough to have their own phone at that time. The number was 21106 and being there when it actually rang was guaranteed to provoke a panic in me.

I remember the huge fridge which men walked into to hang up carcases. I was always worried in case some hapless butcher was trapped inside the frosty interior. Strangely, I was never bothered by the lethal cleavers or sharp knives lying about, or the antiquated mincing machine.

Sometimes I was allowed to help with the sausage machine and recall being taught how to make links of sausage. I then hung them up on a hook suspended from the broad shiny rail above the open counter. My dad had to lift me up as I was too small to reach.

During the war when the younger men were called up, the shop was short staffed. I helped to pluck chickens until my fingers were sore.

My dad always brought me a treat, my favourite being 'Uncle Sherbet'. This was a little man made of sweeties full of sherbet, all pretty sugared almond colours enclosed in cellophane. Christmas was the busiest times for the butchers, but it was also the coldest, when the market was freezing. Icy draughts whistled down the long alleys and my dad resorted to wearing the kind of breeches and leather gaiters which farmers wore in those days to keep warm. Nowadays efficient heaters are much in evidence, though they cannot be over used because of all the fresh meat on sale. When you come to visit our impressive shopping palaces, I hope you will not neglect the Grainger Market. It is a grand place to shop, with plenty of bargains, a friendly atmosphere, space and well displayed goods. All the features of the modern shopping centres, but the Grainger Market had them first.

Jane Smailes

The best market was of course the Grainger Market. Friendly staff in the shops and on the stalls made the visit to the market more of an experience, with their banter and ability to use 'real' measurements (pounds and ounces) with real value money savings.

Graham Falcon

The Penny Market was good value for money, although I found the surrounding shops hard to bear - birds hanging in butchers' shops with the feathers still on and pigs hanging upside down with oranges in their mouths. Oh, and the smells….!

Margaret Hogan

We used to go regularly to the Grainger Market and my mam used to buy the special offer meat packs from the butchers. I remember dead birds hanging up and I still hate the smell of raw meat. There was a café upstairs in the market and we always used to visit Robinson's Pet Shop where there was a talking parrot.

Sue Jeffs

TOP) ROMANCE IN THE BUTCHERS' AISLE? 1970S. ABOVE) INCREDIBLE PRICES IN THE 1980S. LEFT) AN ABIDING MEMORY FOR MOST PEOPLE - CHICKENS AND RABBITS HUNG OUTSIDE WARNER & HURST.

QUIET, GRAND SPLENDOUR IN THE CITY CENTRE, CENTRAL ARCADE.

CENTRAL ARCADE

The Central Exchange, built in 1837, was another of Grainger's masterpieces; a triangular, triple domed design located between Grey Street, Market Street and Grainger Street. It wasn't until 1906 that it was developed into a shopping arcade after a devastating fire; its former life being that of a commercial exchange, newsroom and art gallery. The intricate floor consisted of glass tiles which allowed light to filter through to service tunnels below; however recent replacements during renovation work no longer let through the light, which is a shame for any Geordie borrowers or moles.

Walking through the arcade now you are still transported to a more genteel era, as despite the revamp with its lovely tiles, the interior is much unchanged from its 1906 opening; which is always useful if you fancy doing abit of time travelling and escape the hubbub of the modern world.

ROYAL ARCADE

It seems Richard Grainger did not always have the midas touch. His Royal Arcade built in 1832 is sadly no longer to be found on Pilgrim Street. This classical Greek revival building housing shops and offices was the victim of geographical preference, as 'location, location, location' proved ever important and shopping moved further away from the river banks toward Monument and Northumberland Street.

IT'S DIFFICULT TO IMAGINE THAT THIS AREA IS NOW OCCUPIED BY SWAN HOUSE ROUNDABOUT AND THE CENTRAL MOTORWAY. ROYAL ARCADE.

The poet Sir John Betjeman said 'There is no industrial city in Britain with such a distinguished heritage of classic town planning as Newcastle and one of its highlights is the Royal Arcade'. Clearly the powers that be did not agree. In 1963, the Arcade was dismantled to make way for the not so classical architecture of Swan House Roundabout and the Central Motorway. There were plans to rebuild the arcade but this never happened. A replica was built underneath Swan House but just like the original it never really took off and was demolished in 2002: it would appear this part of town just isn't well suited to retail outlets.

LEAZES ARCADE

A Dickensian style shopping centre in a former Jewish Synagogue you say? How very 1980s! The promotional materials for Leazes Arcade promise a 'bubbling Christmas-time atmosphere all the year round' and perhaps takes a dig at its unnamed but probably not so distant counterpart by referencing 'a refreshing alternative to large impersonal shopping centres'. Hmmm, as Leazes Arcade was situated just off Percy Street who could they possibly mean…?

If there was a Christmas-time atmosphere then someone must have left those Christmas lights on too long as a fire broke out in 1989, which wreaked such havoc that only the external walls remained. All traces of friendly Dickensian shopping were burnt to a crisp. Bah humbug.

And what has become of Leazes Arcade now you wonder? Take an educated guess as it is happening all over the city…yes that's right, the Arcade is of course now student accommodation.

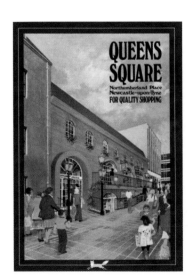

QUEENS SQUARE

The 1980s must have been the era for building quaint shopping arcades that attempted to hark back to more genteel days, as in addition to Leazes Arcade, Queens Square was another new kid on the shopping block. Describing itself as 'quality retailing' with a 'tasteful village square theme'.

The tasteful village square has now been corrupted: the site is now occupied by an amusement arcade.

LAMPLIGHTER CAFE IN LEAZES ARCADE

HANDYSIDE ARCADE

Although it was built in 1906 it wasn't until the 1960s that the Handyside Arcade really swung into life, to the extent that it was regarded as Tyneside's answer to Carnaby Street. Named after its founder, George Handyside, the arcade was a development that was used as a barracks during World War 1 before becoming derelict during the depression years and rising like a phoenix in the 1960s to become a haven for the burgeoning teenage scene; a tradition that passed on through the 1970s and into the 1980s when music fans congregated for the day and the smell of incense filled the air.

The structure was controversially demolished in the late 1980s to make way for the comparatively bland and boring Eldon Gardens. The original roof trusses of the Handyside were incorporated into the new structure so part of it still lives on, as well as in the hearts and minds of certain generations.

I bought two beautiful white linen dresses at the Handyside Boutique. Linen was very fashionable in the sixties and I loved them. I wore them to a BBQ on holiday whilst in Majorca and got Sangria all over one and the other I brought home in the suitcase along with a bottle of red wine. Unfortunately the bottle smashed and ruined all of my clothes that were in the case. They have to be the most expensive dresses I have ever bought!

Margaret Dinsdale

The Handyside Arcade attracted all sorts. 'Fynd' and various second hand shops made it a magnet for hippies and punks alike. It was at the Kard Bar that I bought my first *Viz*, despite being a 'minor' at the time. You could still wander about on the upper level, but there was often the risk of bumping into undesirables who, like ourselves, had no good reason to be there. There was always a sad, haunted feel to the place, especially the pet shop with its animals painted on the outside.

Sarah Hall

HIPPY CENTRAL –
HANDYSIDE ARCADE

MONUMENT MALL

When exactly did shopping arcades become malls? In Newcastle it would appear to be around 1990 when the Monument Mall opened its doors. Was the name due to the creeping Americanisation of English language, or perhaps the city was all 'arcaded' out, or maybe the use of an alliterative title was simply too appealing? Whichever it was, the design of the mall was perhaps ill-judged as just twenty-one years later the mall was subject to a refurbishment to the tune of £15 million. As the atrium and walkways were filled in it became less of a mall and more just a building with shops in that you access from the street. I'm guessing they couldn't drop the mall bit though as then it would just be Monument, and we already have one of those…

THE SITE THAT FORMS THE JUNCTION OF NORTHUMBERLAND STREET AND BLACKETT STREET HAS SEEN MANY GUISES. FROM LOWE AND MOORHOUSE, TO BURTON'S MENSWEAR, MONUMENT MALL – THE MALL NOW FILLED IN WITH TK MAXX, A JEWELLERS ON THE CORNER AND THE BOTANIST RESTAURANT.

Newcastle upon Tyne

When I was young a trip to Newcastle always meant a trip to Eldon Square and the thing that sticks in my mind are the seats that were shaped like pencils...at least I think they were seats, I just remember climbing on them as though that is what they were meant for!

Steven Duke

ELDON SQUARE

It's hard to believe Eldon Square is now over forty years old. The controversial decision to pull down the majority of John Dobson's historic square, which was argued by some to be of national architectural significance, still grates for some Geordies who did not appreciate the graceful 'old' Eldon Square being ransacked to create the young whippersnapper modern market mecca of 'new' Eldon Square, or just plain Eldon Square as we now know it. The King is dead, long live the King and all that. Eldon Square is now very much at the heart of Newcastle shopping and has itself been the subject of much transformation over the years. Remember the giant pencils? Remember the Green Market? Remember the water features or spaceship café? Remember the giant red 'E's? Maybe these pictures will jog your memory....

BELOW LEFT) THE FAMOUS BAINBRIDGE'S 'SPACE SHIP' CAFE. BELOW RIGHT) THE ENTRANCE TO ELDON SQUARE IN THE EARLY 90S.

I was working in Newcastle during the excavations for the Metro line and the building of Eldon Square Shopping Centre. The office windows looked out onto what was Binns corner and down the length of Grainger Street, other office windows opened out onto Grainger Arcade. Occasionally when it was hot, we could step through these windows onto the ledge that ran the length of the Arcade so you could really see how lovely the roof and ornate tiles were; a secret world where you could look down on shoppers going into Windows Music Shop.

I remember the day Eldon Square opened, we were so excited to see this new shopping experience and talked for hours about what it would be like inside. Fortunately, we happened to be having an unusually quiet week at work so when the Secretary told a colleague and myself we could have an extra fifteen minutes for our lunch break to check it out we couldn't believe our luck.

I still remember how excited we were when we went into the entrance and up the escalator: lots of 'oohs' and 'look at that's'! All these fantastic shops under cover then up another escalator to a fitness centre so modern it was like seeing the future. We couldn't wait for Saturday when we could explore everything at our leisure.

Pat Rogerson

When Eldon Square opened in 1976, the concept of a shopping mall and shopping as a leisure activity was encouraged. This was catered for with seating areas, children's areas with the famous giant pencils and café areas to snack in. You could window shop indoors on a rainy day and use the multi-storey car park close by on Percy Street.

Elspeth Rutter

The husband of the couple I babysit for used to be picked up from school by his gran when he was four or five and taken as a treat to play on the 'pencils'. This was an area at the back of Bainbridge's (John Lewis). This area was a dedicated play area for children. The family have an original leaflet with a picture showing the pencils and Philip in his school uniform playing on them. Philip is now forty-four!

Patricia Ward Lynn

How can anyone forget the pencils in Eldon Square? An icon and a favourite place to scramble for any child of the 70s! And not too far from the UFO - Bainbridge's coffee shop, jutting out into the mall. Fantastic. It was a sad day when that came down.

Kirsty Ferry

RIGHT) ENJOYING AN ICE CREAM IN ELDON SQUARE IN 1986, THE BRICK PLANTERS THROUGHOUT THE SHOPPING CENTRE GAVE OFF AN EARTHY SMELL. BELOW) THE MEMORABLE 'ES' ON NORTHUMBERLAND STREET.

Eldon Square NEWCASTLE

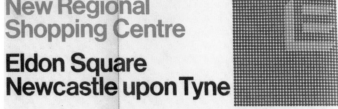

New Regional Shopping Centre
Eldon Square
Newcastle upon Tyne

TOM YELLOWLEY

BOTH PAGES, CLOCKWISE FROM TOP LEFT. 1) A PROMOTIONAL POSTCARD FOR ELDON SQUARE FEATURING THE 'PENCILS', THE FOUNTATIONS AND 'SPACE SHIP' CAFE. 2) FROM THE PROMOTIONAL MATERIAL FOR 'NEW' ELDON SQUARE, 1975. 3) AN AERIAL VIEW OF THE CENTRE, LATES 70S. 4) 'LOOK MAM, THAT'S WHERE THE PENCILS ARE, 1982. 5) THE REFURBISHED AREA OF THE SOUTH END OF ELDON SQUARE IN 2011. 6) A 70S MAP OF ELDON SQUARE. 7)THOSE PENCILS AGAIN, 1976.

ELDON GARDENS

Eldon Square has morphed over the years, the biggest change being the addition of Eldon Gardens which these days is less of a garden and more a mishmash of independent retailers and vacant units. The Garden celebrated its twenty-fifth anniversary in 2014; though pruning has taken place over time as much of its original mall floorspace has now been consumed by a venture that always does well in Newcastle: a pub.

In 2018 the small mall was 85% vacant, and the council and the owners are considering closing it all together. Perhaps another one bites the dust?

GREAT NORTHERN BRANDS AND BUSINESSES SOME GONE BUT NOT FORGOTTEN...

FENWICK

Think of a Newcastle department store, think of Fenwick's, as that's how the majority of us refer to it, who knows where we got that 's' from. Whilst the other great names of department stores in the region have been sucked into corporate brands from elsewhere, Fenwick's is still Fenwick's - as it has always been and is a department store born and bred in Newcastle.

Mr John James Fenwick opened his Newcastle store in 1882 at 5 Northumberland Street, converting a doctor's house in a residential area into a shop selling fabric, silk goods, dresses and mantles (a cloak or shawl to you and me) basically he sold ladieswear. Since time immemorial women have generally been the shoppers in the household and ambitious Mr Fenwick spotted a business opportunity by targeting his goods at the ladies of Newcastle. They did not disappoint and proved his instinct to be correct. Within three years the business had moved to larger premises at 37/38 Northumberland Street, expanding further in later years to acquire number 40, where Fenwick's remains today. A Newcastle institution renowned for quality goods and, since 1971, its famous Christmas window, the store is likely to be a feature of Newcastle life for many more years to come.

FENWICK'S, 1898.

A Wedding in the Spring?

MANY OF THE MOST memorable weddings have been dressed by Fenwick's and for spring we already have an enchanting collection of bridal gowns and head-dresses in a wide price range. Why not come in today— we are ready to help the bride in every way to look her radiant best.

FRENCH SALON
AND FIRST FLOOR

★
If an account would assist your shopping, our Bureau, First Floor is ready to arrange it.

A CITY IN ITSELF

Northumberland Street was still used as the A1 when I was a child, so not so pleasant to shop on. Probably my favourite shop was Fenwick's, which was just about affordable (compared with Bainbridge's, which wasn't). From being a child I loved the Christmas window displays. All credit to the shop that it still shows such imagination each year. My only 'complaint' now is that the music is far too loud as you walk past!

Anne Nelson

As a child growing up in the 1980's Fenwick's toy department was nothing short of heaven: every imaginable toy and cuddly animal you could dream of and I'm sure it filled the whole top floor, not like the comparably meagre offering of today. Perhaps the additions of Hamleys on Northumberland Street or out of town shopping such as Toys 'R' Us near the Metro Centre made Fenwick's reduce their toy floorspace...or maybe it just feels like it shrunk as I got bigger!

Victoria Richards

When I was a kid, any visit to Eldon Square had to include a visit to Fenwick's , particularly the magnificent toy department where I usually spent all of my pocket money by adding to my collection of *Star Wars* toys. I remember when I was around six or seven I entered a competition where you had to answer some *Star Wars* related questions and invent a new character to replace Yoda as it was just after the *Empire Strikes Back* had been released: I won first prize! My childhood dreams were made when I won a toy AT-AT which seemed huge to me back then but then again so did the whole toy department! I now take my own children to Fenwick's toy department but it is definitely not the same as it used to be when I was growing up.

Steven Duke

1987.

1989.

As a child going shopping in Newcastle was always an adventure. Whether it was by bus which meant making at least one connection and the journey taking around one and a half hours or by car which still took almost an hour after having found a convenient side street to park in (and then remembering the location of said street). It felt like travelling to the 'big city' which in those days, to me, it was. It was always so exciting around Christmas time when the days were short and the lights so colourful and bright and most of the shops were so warm. Glitter and tinsel welcomed everyone inside. Fenwick's window, in those days, really was a sight to behold. And it always seemed to always have a Christmas theme (unlike today). It was not unusual to stand and queue for what seemed like hours to get a glimpse of Santa and his elves and reindeer. Inside the store the toy display a few floors up was simply amazing and I could spend all day looking in awe at what was available, whilst making a mental list of everything that took my fancy...not that very much of it would end up in my Santa sack.

Simon Carey

I remember my children waiting eagerly for the first view of Fenwick's Christmas window each year. The excitement started mounting after the October half term when the windows would be papered over and they waited impatiently for the big reveal of that year's display. From fairy tales, to books such as *The Snowman* and biblical nativities, to futuristic aliens - each was discussed at the family meal table and the merits considered. It has become such a part of Christmas it now seems impossible to start shopping until Fenwick's window is open. I remember an aunt from Devon proudly announcing that she had all her Christmas shopping done by the end of September - bought and wrapped! We were amazed - how could she possibly think of Christmas so early? Christmas only truly begins in our family after Fenwick's window display is revealed.

Babs Trevitt

VISITING FENWICK'S CHRISTMAS WINDOW HAS BECOME A FAMILY TRADITION IN THE RUN UP TO CHRISTMAS. NOW FEATURING COUNTDOWNS, CELEBRITIES AND ARTIFICAL SNOW ON NORTHUMBERLAND STREET - SPRAYED FROM THE ROOF OF THE BUILDING FOOLING CHRISTMAS SHOPPERS.

A CITY IN ITSELF

COME TO Fenwick's at the heart of Newcastle and you will discover why we're one of the major department stores in the country. Five huge floors offer you a comprehensive mix of fine shopping from an extensive range of cosmetics and fragrances to our wonderland of toys – loved by generations of children; from hi-tec television, audio and video equipment to the fashion ranges on which we have built our reputation; from the mouth-watering food in our seven restaurants and in our magnificent Delicatessen to a sparkling selection of china and giftware. It's all here waiting for you in the city of Fenwick.

Fenwick

Entrances from Northumberland Street, Eldon Square Shopping Precinct and Blackett Street.

CLOCKWISE FROM TOP LEFT (BOTH PAGES) 1) LOOKING DOWN NORTHUMBERLAND STREET IN THE EARLY 80S, BURTON MENSWEAR STILL ON THE JUNCTION WITH BLACKETT STREET. 2) FENWICK'S 90S ADVERT. 3)LIT UP FOR CHRISTMAS, 1985. 4)1900 – THE LARGEST SIGNBOARD EVER ERECTED IN NEWCASTLE. 5) FENWICK'S SHOP FRONT IN THE LATE 1900S. 6)GREAT STYLES ON DISPLAY IN 1968, STRANGE THAT THE MANNIQUINS ARE HEADLESS. 7) KIDS DRAGGED AROUND FENWICK'S SALE, 1993.

THE LARGEST SIGNBOARD EVER ERECTED IN NEWCASTLE

Fenwick's was a treat at Christmas, they had a payment in instalments system so you felt you could afford more as you were given longer to pay it off. I remember visiting Fenwick's on a Saturday for tea and scones but my main memory is of the place being full of smoke from cigarettes!

Denise Gibson

Fenwick's used to close at 1pm on a Saturday! Imagine that now!

Derek Ferguson

The premier department store in Newcastle was of course Fenwick's. We would go into the coffee shop for coffee and a ciggie for Mam then through the perfumery where glamorous girls stood behind Chanel counters. There were wonderful handbags and haberdashery and a marvellous delicatessen area to buy Blue Mountain coffee at a reasonable price. Bainbridge's was excellent too. Slightly below that came Binns and then Farnons where you went for everyday stuff like tea towels.

Sue Holdroyd

CLOCKWISE FROM TOP. 1) A COLOURFUL FENWICKS, 1962. 2) MORE HEADLESS FASHIONS, LATE 50S. 3) TRAFFIC BUSY ON NORTHUMBERLAND STREET, 1971.

BAINBRIDGE

Or Bainbridge's as most of us refer to it – that mysterious 's' is back again…

It was 1838 and the ways of the shopping world were very different from today. Goods didn't have price labels so you had to barter instead, making shopping quite an unfair experience if you were rotten at haggling and overall a tedious and time consuming exercise. Then along came pricing pioneer Emerson Muschamp Bainbridge, champion of fixed charges, empowering customers to know exactly how much goods would place them out of pocket and changing the face of retailing in Newcastle (and beyond) forever.

Shopping in this period also involved visiting individual retailers for specific goods; meaning you could be out a good part of the day by the time you had bartered your way around a number of outlets. It was just as well that women in those days tended to be 'housewives' as there would not have been enough hours in the day for effective haggling and holding down employment too. Recognising the inconvenience, Mr Bainbridge streamlined shopping further by revolutionizing the practice of selling a number of goods in one shop. By 1849, weekly takings in his store were recorded by department; thus making Newcastle the birthplace of possibly the world's first department store and giving weary shoppers not only their goods but also the gift of time.

A pioneer of his period, the founder made Bainbridge an institution that valued its employees as well as its consumers. Shop assistants who had fallen on hard times benefitted from the Albert House Benevolent Society which was a subscription scheme that was then matched by the company. Any current or former employee in need could benefit from this, even if they had subscribed or not.

'SHOPPING BAG LADIES' MEET FOR A CHAT - BAINBRIDGE SEEN FROM THE ENTRANCE TO CENTRAL ARCADE ON MARKET STREET, 1930S.

Poorer members of society were also assisted during the depression years as agents for the company collected payments in instalments from those in less affluent areas. How very altruistic, what a lovely company! Well yes…but this was also an effective marketing technique to ensure sales remained up and that the Bainbridge name remained in people's minds…which clearly worked as the business continued to thrive despite the difficult economic times.

In October 1977, the shop relocated from its home on Market Street to its current site in Eldon Square. Although the business joined forces with the John Lewis partnership in 1953, it did not change its name until 2002. This followed a store staff vote that it should take the name of the partnership rather than retain that of its founder. Sad times and the end of an era for some, though for many in the North East it is still referred to as Bainbridge's… and probably always will be.

When I learned to sew in the fifties I was shopping for fabrics which I mainly bought from the Silk Shop opposite the Odeon on Pilgrim Street. This eventually moved into Bainbridge's on Market Street. The Silk Shop was wonderful with a much bigger selection than you would get today. There were rows and rows of rolls of cloth to choose from. Most mums and grandmas sewed then. Everyone had a button box or jar to reuse, this is called recycling these days! Buttons from France were highly sought after and reused many times, they were much more exciting than our UK selection.

Elspeth Rutter

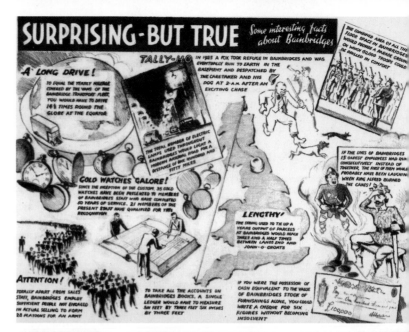

CLOCKWISE FROM TOP. 1) INTERESTING BAINBRIDGE FACTS, 1938. 2) PACKING UP TO MOVE INTO ELDON SQUARE, 1976. 3) 50S ADVERT FOR SHEEPSKIN COATS 4) THE NEW HOME IN ELDON SQUARE, EARLY 2000S. 5)KITCHENWARE DEPARTMENT, 70S.

JOHN LEWIS PARTNERSHIP

BAINBRIDGE NEWCASTLE

TOM YELLOWLEY

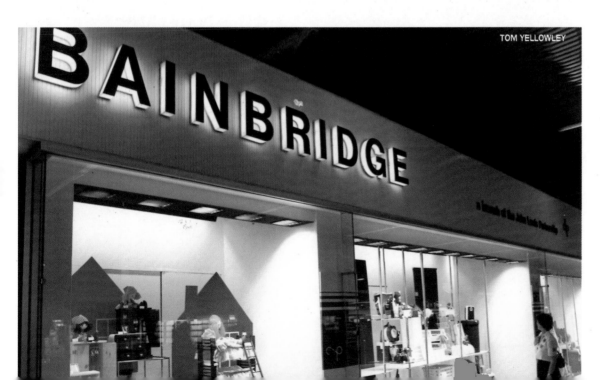

Make hay while the snow falls
in this delightful Continental Sheepskin Coat
of perfectly blended supple skins. 29 Gns.
Complete outfit from our Fashion Floor.

Bainbridges.

FIRST FLOOR

A BEAUTIFUL BUILDING ON MARKET STREET, 1912. NEXT PAGE) THE SAME AREA IN LESS SALUBRIOUS TIMES.

BINNS

Imagine the shopping heaven of two large department stores side by side; well this was a reality in Newcastle when Binns and Bainbridge were neighbours on Market Street. Being a Sunderland company and with successful stores already operating across the North East, Binns was one of the only Mackem businesses Geordies welcomed with open arms. It opened its doors in 1929 on the site formerly occupied by drapers Coxon & Co. on the corner of Market and Grey Street.

Generations of families have since argued over where Binns was located in town and the argument can now be settled - it had two premises. The confusion arises as when Bainbridge relocated to Eldon Square, Binns moved into the old Bainbridge premises, which will be the site younger generations recall. This store had entrances on Market Street, Grainger Street and the Bigg Market and was three times larger than its previous premises. The store closed in 1996 and potentially its size or location may have ultimately brought its downfall. Absorbed into the House of Fraser empire, which now had a branch in the Metro Centre, those in Fraser HQ perhaps recognised NewcastleGateshead as a location long before it became a marketing venture to promote the region. Two outlets in one geographical area was therefore deemed too much and given that Fenwick

and 'Bainbridge' were already muscle men in toon, it made good business sense to choose a presence in the Metro Centre if a decision came down to one site over the other. Furthermore 'location, location, location' may once again have played a part as Newcastle's shopping epicentre shifted to Eldon Square and Northumberland Street; making the Binns site more of a trek than most shoppers may like, particularly given the North East weather.

My mother mainly shopped at Binns and she met her Scottish friends for coffee at their tea rooms. They sometimes had models (one was Norma James) walking among the tables, showing the new season's clothes.

Elspeth Rutter

My mum and dad had an account at Binns Department store in Newcastle, which meant that my sister and I had to get all our clothes form the children's department there. Ladybird vests, Startrite shoes - all pretty old fashioned, but made to last. We always had 'Mabel' serve us, and I was fascinated by the shoe measuring machine, which seemed enormous and also a bit scary. When I got to thirteen my mum 'allowed' me to pick my own clothes... so long as they were from Binns children's department and so long as Mabel served me. I got my first pair of Clark's Horoscope shoes from there and felt really grown up as they had a tiny heel and were patent leather! I went through the whole of my childhood wishing that my parents had an account at Bainbridge's - that shop seemed much more exciting.

Alison Jobey

Binns was my favourite department store and seemed to sell just about anything and everything. My parents had an account there; any goods bought on this account were settled at the end of the month. Whenever a purchase was made the counter staff would send the details up to their accounts office via torpedo! The paperwork was inserted into a cylinder and this was then placed into a set of pipework which carried it (on a jet of air) to 'accounts'. A wait of about five minutes then took place before a receipt was returned in exactly the same way. There was a myriad of pipework like this around the store and it really was cutting edge.

Simon Carey

TOP) OUTSIDE BINNS RESTAURANT ON MARKET STREET - NOW HARRY'S BAR. ABOVE)1940S INTERIOR AT BINN'S.

In 1989 my daughter Miriam was just one year old. For some reason I was rushing through the centre of Newcastle and seemed to take a short cut through Binns Department Store. I was passing through the basement or what I remember to be a connecting tunnel or passage and there was a cot full of wonderful soft toys. I plunged my hand in arbitrarily and plucked out a small white Polar Bear. The bear became Miriam's constant companion and was eventually dubbed "Snowy" - it was thrust at every unsuspecting relative and passer-by and was even enshrined in a locket around my daughter's neck. "Snowy" has survived all manner of travel and accommodation and developed a lore all of his own - he survives today with a slightly worn rodent like appearance. What if I hadn't taken that short cut through Binns?

Chris Phipps

I felt the closing of Binns department store was a great loss. When Bainbridge's was on the corner of Grainger Street it was next door on Market Street, but later transferred into Bainbridge's site when the latter moved into the Eldon Square complex. It was never the same after that! It was a shop which could appeal to people on all incomes – not too expensive and with an excellent range of goods.

Anne Nelson

TOP) MIRIAM WITH BINNS WELL-TRAVELLED 'SNOWY'. RIGHT) THE JUNCTION OF GREY STREET AND MARKET STREET – NEIGHBOURS BINN'S AND BAINBRIDGE.

FARNONS

John Farnon was an Irish linen importer who founded the Farnons department store in Nun Street in the 1800s. Mr Farnon was somewhat of a celebrity in Newcastle at the time, being also a Councillor, Justice of the Peace and serving on Newcastle School Board. Alas however he may have spread himself too short as his retail venture was failing by the 1920s. Fortunately commercial representative and draper John Norman Howard stepped in to save the day and rescued the business from administration, doing a grand job of it too as it was retained as a family business until 1959.

One of the quirks of the store was having premises on both sides of Nun Street, which became one of their straplines: *Both Sides of Nun Street and Newgate Street too!* In addition to *Try Farnons first* which reflected the company's awareness that it was often a last resort for customers who couldn't find what they wanted elsewhere, so ended up in Farnons last…and then found exactly what they wanted in the first place.

Farnons prided itself on being a value for money store offering everything from school uniforms to curtains and corsetry; it knew

its place in the Newcastle department store pecking order and targeted its market accordingly.

Michael Howard, John Norman Howard's grandson, recalls the retail environment of the time as very much that of the 'Are you being served' ilk with employees referring to each other as Mr or Miss etc - all very formal by today's standards where perfect strangers can see your first name emblazoned on your name badge. Behind the scenes there were also different dining arrangements depending on the superiority of staff. The directors were served by waitresses in fancy rooms adorned with heavy wooden panels and table cloths, the buyers dined in a slightly less but still grand room where traders would come to show their wares, while department heads had their scran in a third room to themselves. All very different to the informal canteen culture of today – and that's if employers still have feeding facilities as a fridge and microwave could be classed as lunchtime luxury now.

The business was also one to use the 'Lansom' system of payment; a series of tubes throughout the store sent money whizzing from the customer service desk to cashiers elsewhere. In Farnons case this could even mean in another building as tubes ran under the road at Nun Street: heaven forbid they were ever to get stuck! This was the golden era of customer service: cash transactions were taken first to enable Mrs Cannybody-Customerservice to wrap your goods for you before your change whizzed magically back to you through the Lansom tubes. The days of your change being thrown back in your face by a disgruntled Saturday girl, keen only to get her queue down so she can bagsy that one dodgy microwave on her lunchbreak were well in the future.

It was also the era before the Disability Discrimination Act meaning people didn't consider the need for accessibility; which was just as well as Farnons was a myriad of levels with seemingly random steps up and down throughout the split level store.

Retailing itself was a very different beast compared to today. There were no Sunday opening hours but shops closed for half a day on Wednesdays – any family wedding of those working in the retail trade therefore had to be held on a Wednesday afternoon. Saturdays were the busiest day of the week, meaning if you were a football fan working in retail you were basically screwed: there could be no nipping off for the 3pm kick off as it was very much a case of 'all hands on deck' for hectic Saturday trading.

The working hours of five and a half days a week effectively meant you had forsaken your leisure time for a job in retail; it's a wonder how shop workers managed to do any shopping themselves!

Just like most of the other regional department stores, Farnons was eventually bought by a national company and finally closed its doors in the 1990s. As another local legend bit the dust, shoppers were left scratching their heads as to where they should now head to as a last resort…

PREVIOUS PAGE) FARNONS SALE, 1990S.
THIS PAGE) LOOKING ALONG NUN STREET TOWARDS GRAINGER STREET, 50S.

Farnons was the place to buy net curtains, I still remember buying them by the yard. The shop was always full and the smell of the nets was lovely. Most people had net curtains in the sixties and there were many patterns to choose from. Now it's all blinds - how times have changed. My lasting memory of Farnons is the creaking of the wood floors and the big old fashioned lift.

Margaret Dinsdale

Every August my mother took our school uniform grant for me and my four siblings to Farnon's. I remember the payment being put in tubes and whizzed off to the cashiers, who then sent back any change.

Sue Jeffs

I remember visiting Farnons in Newcastle in the early 1970s. I was always bored in this shop, the only items bought for me were school uniform (the 'ladybird' label) otherwise it was dull household things. The highlight for me was watching the metal tubes travelling around the tracks taking bills and money to the office, and the old fashioned lift with the wrought iron doors.

Judith Newman

Farnons was good for cheaper underwear and stockings; mother was an expert bargain hunter so these prices were more suited to her needs. The war had honed that skill in most mothers.

Patricia Bensdorp-Clark

TOP) TWIN SETS, BUT NO PEARLS - WORKERS IN FARNONS. ABOVE) ANOTHER SAL IN FARNON'S IN THE 80S.

J.G. WINDOWS

If you're from the North East where would you go for your first instrument if you were a budding Buddy Holly, maybe Mozart, 'just-about' John Lennon or novice Noel Gallagher?

J.G Windows of course! The flagship Newcastle store remains the go-to place for all music related items and has been so for over 100 years. In 2008 the firm celebrated its centenary of business, making it older than the renowned HMV music empire, which opened its doors thirteen years after J.G Windows in 1921. This makes the company one of the UK's longest established music stores and a bona fide Newcastle business success story. After all can you think of any other shop that has been in the Central Arcade as long? No, because there isn't one; J.G. Windows has defied the retail churn.

The founder, James Gale Windows, a former music seller and pianoforte dealer's assistant, opened the shop in Central Arcade in 1908 selling musical instruments, printed and recorded music. By the early 1920s, James' first son Maurice joined the company and business expanded by opening a further shop in Darlington; second son Hedley joined later and ran the music department in the Newcastle shop, making the business a full family affair until James' death in 1933. The two brothers continued to run the shop despite enlisting and fighting for their country during the Second World War alongside a number of their employees.

By the 1960s, the Newcastle store was the biggest music shop in the country outside Oxford Street, London. Hedley's son James Bowen

Windows joined the business in 1961 after training as a Chartered Accountant and ran the company until it was purchased in 2006 by three current and former employees.

The business remains a success as the range of products and services have adapted over time; from the publication of Tyneside songs with piano arrangements by Charles Ernest Catcheside-Warrington in 1912 to DJ equipment and an online presence today. Indeed the changes in musical fashions is evidenced by demand for instruments dropping in the early 1990s boy band era; to customers clamouring for guitars through the grunge and indie music phases; to a more recent spike in demand for ukuleles.

An excellent reputation and ability to remain at the forefront of musical instruments and equipment has enabled further growth and expansion of the business, with the company being the only one in the country to provide the full variety of musical products as a general music shop.

The shop has always provided a very personal service, which keeps customers coming back. Helen Mawson, who has worked for the company for thirty-five years, remembers Mr Ribeiro, a Portuguese chain-smoking gentleman who frequented the store in the days when smoking was allowed in shops (ashtrays were even provided on the counters). He would spend hours in the shop listening to music, therefore when the 'no smoking' laws were introduced the business was keen not to deter their much valued client. Rather than lose his custom the company arranged for CDs to be sent instead to his room at the Imperial Hotel in Jesmond, where he could happily listen to their offerings and still chain-smoke to his heart's content.

Famous faces have also succumbed to the Windows charm: many actors staying at the nearby Turks Head Hotel, whilst appearing in plays at the Theatre Royal, paid the shop a visit. Barry Humphries visiting as Dame Edna Everage was one of the particular highlights! Other famous customers have included the band Lindisfarne, Sheena Easton, Rowan Atkinson, Placido Domingo, Andre Previn and Joan Sutherland.

Though staff may no longer greet people wearing bowler hats as they did when the store first opened, the friendly familiarity means this shop is likely to continue providing a service to future musicians of the North East for many years to come.

When I was fifteen in the late fifties I applied for a Saturday job in Windows in the Central Arcade. I was so excited when I was chosen and looked forward to Saturday all week. In fact I would have worked for nothing as I loved it so much. At that time it was the place for teenagers to meet and gangs of young people hung around all day. There were booths to listen to records and they were always packed, even though most of them enjoyed listening but couldn't afford to buy. Mr Windows was very kind to his staff and treated us all to afternoon tea at the Tyne Hotel every week. We were served by waitresses wearing black dresses and white aprons which made us feel quite posh! One Saturday a young man came in and asked if I would go out with him. We married and were together for over fifty years so I had a lot to thank that shop for and it's still in the same spot today.

Judith McCoy

As I learned to play the violin whilst at school I used to frequent Windows in the Central Arcade; it was lovely to see on my return to the North East that the shop is still there! The arcade is probably one of the most underrated buildings in the city centre.

Anne Nelson

JACKSON THE TAILOR

In 1906, Moses Jacobson opened a tailoring shop on Clayton Street. This small shop sowed the seed for what was to become one of the oldest English menswear brands and created a nationwide retailing empire that was regarded as the go-to place for suits for special occasions. It was so famous it was even mentioned in an episode of *The Likely Lads*!

I remember in the late 60s when I used to visit Jackson the Tailor on Clayton Street. In those days suits were all made to measure and not off the peg.

Jane Armstrong

My favourite personal shopping experience was going to Jackson the Tailor's in Northumberland Street after saving up to order my first ever made-to-measure suit. After picking the colour and material from a very large book of samples, the number of the chosen selection was written down on the order form; then a well-spoken voice said to me 'May I take Sir's measurements now please?' That was an experience in itself but all carried out with the upmost courtesy throughout; even if I was a little bemused when asked 'Which side does Sir dress on?' when doing the trousers. When picking up the suit later, I tried it on to make sure everything was satisfactory, which of course it was, it was perfect in all respects. I settled my bill and left feeling proud as a peacock with my first ever made-to-measure suit in a Jackson the Tailor's bag; I have never forgotten how good the service and courtesy was.

Tim McMahon

'What's happening to me?'

'I've always thought I was as easy to please as the next man, Mr. Jackson,' said this young fellow. 'But something seems to have come over me since I got that suit from you.'
'Why should that be, I wonder?' I said, smiling.
'Well,' he said, 'it was so much better than anything I'd ever had before, that it made me dissatisfied with the rest of my clothes. I found myself buying smarter shirts and ties—being particular about shoes. Then the chaps where I work began coming to me for advice, and treating me as if I was a senior.

What's happening to me?
As I told him—something to be pleased about. His standard of dressing has gone up. I've seen it happen over and over again with our customers. We introduce them to suits with our own special cut and the rest follows. What a gain it is —in confidence, progress towards success, popularity in the office and out of it! Think I'm exaggerating? Come to us for your next suit—and watch it happen to you.

Prices (tomeasure or ready tailored) 8, 10 or 12 gns., and you can pay 'out-of-income' if you prefer it.

Jackson the tailor

TOP) JACKSON THE TAILOR'S ON NORTHUMBERLAND STREET. FAR RIGHT) AT ITS HOME AT THE JUNCTION OF CLAYTON STREET AND FENKLE STREET. RIGHT) 'WHAT'S HAPPENING TO ME?' A NATTY AD FOR JACKSON'S.

CALLERS

Callers? You mean Callers Pegasus? No you young thing! Although the travel agents were part of the wider company I'm talking about Callers 'the home of good furnishing', donator of clocks to the city, trailblazer of Christmas windows and fire-starter extraordinaire: unfortunately the Callers fire of 1969 is now the most vivid memory for those who can recall the brand in its heyday.

The firm were renowned for their furniture displays, with floor space set up as rooms to showcase the goods in a 'real environment'. Prior to the fire, the building had large recessed windows which meant you could walk into the display; as these were arcade style you could even do this when the shop was closed!

Those of a certain age are likely to remember where they were when they heard about the 1969 fire, a blaze so fierce it nearly brought down Northumberland Street and cost Callers £2million at the time. The blaze started from smoke from one of the mechanical toys in the Christmas window display on 30 November 1969; the irony being that the Christmas displays Callers had been famous for created the fire that the company then became famous for…

ABOVE) TACKLING THE CALLERS FIRE ON SAVILLE ROW, 1969. NEXT PAGE, CLOCKWISE FROM TOP LEFT. 1) A CHRISTMAS DISPLAY IN CALLERS WINDOW, COULD THE LIGHTS ON THE TREE BE RESPONSIBLE FOR THE FIRE? 2) HOME INTERIORS DISPLAYED IN CALLERS. 3) AN ADVERT FOR CALLERS - THE 'HOME OF GOOD FURNISHING'.

LOOKING DOWN NEWGATE STREET TOWARD THE CO-OP, 1950S. NEXT PAGE) A WELL-PRESENTED
CO-OP STORE IN STANLEY, CO. DURHAM, 1930S.

CO-OP

Ok so it's not a local business… though founded in Rochdale some southerners may consider it to be a 'northern' brand, but we know that's not the 'proper' north! The Co-op is such a North East institution though it might as well have been born and bred here, hence has made the grade to appear in this section. The organisation features in so many of our memories, from working in the shops to the way we paid (or didn't pay…it wasn't known as the 'steal' works for nothing!) to the fabulous art-deco building that presided over Newgate Street for so many years; the Co-op was a big part of the fabric of northern life.

I remember shopping with my mam in the 50s and 60s. Every Saturday we would go down Darn Crook to the Co-op Coal Office to order more coal, followed by a visit to the butcher next door for a big piece of beef for ten shillings. We then went into the Co-op itself to climb up the wonderful Art Deco staircase. The fabric department was always busy because in those days most women made at least some of their clothes; you could buy pretty summer dress material for 2/11 a yard. This was followed by a visit to the office area to pay off hire purchase or claim dividend - Co-op number 70412! We always had afternoon tea in the Rainbow room.

Sue Holdroyd

My family shopped at the Co-op for groceries as well as clothes. I used to love to walk up and down the stairs using the handrail with the 'little strong men' holding it up!

Patricia Ward Lynn

The Co-op sold 'Stanley Matthews' autographed football boots and 'Cliff Morgan' rugby boots and may have been one of the first companies to try this form of marketing.

Ian Holloway

I remember both Co-op dividend numbers because as a child I would go to the local (Buddle Road, Scotswood Road, High Cross, Adelaide Terrace, Benwell) Co-operative Wholesale Society for blue bagged sugar, bread and other produce for both my mother and aunt; remembering to put the 'cheque' safely into my pocket. You never forget 'divvy' numbers (like service numbers) as the dividend paid for clothing and shoes for all of the family.

Graham Falcon

Looking back, the Co-op was a central factor in our lives. My mother, having no other means of saving than the Co-op dividend, was an avid shopper there. She also believed in the quality of its products though most things were of decent quality in the fifties. The large Co-op store was a short trolley bus ride from where we lived, Stone Street, just off Stanhope Street, though we often walked into town. We would pass Leazes Park where we sometimes hired a rowing boat or fished for minnows with an old stocking for a net.

For the Co-op you had a membership number and with every purchase you got a small paper receipt or cheque as it was called. This gave you the right to a dividend on your purchase which was paid out quarterly. My mam stored the cheques in a milk jug hanging in the kitchen cupboard and counted them religiously before going to the office above the store to have the interest noted in her book. She always knew exactly what was due and looked carefully to see that no errors were made; she had all these tiny slips of paper as evidence of her dedication. In those days you got two shillings dividend for every pound spent at their store; with twenty shillings in the pound this was a generous way to save. A sharp contrast to today's world, where so much is paid by the customer to the stores for credit services. This dividend was paid not only on furniture, clothing etc, but also on food. Mother bought most of her groceries at the local Co-op, which was a very short walk from our flat in Stone Street. There was a baker, a greengrocer and a large grocery, all separate stores next to each other. When you went into the grocers you entered a different world - brown wooden panelling, large polished counters and mirrors. The deep drawers behind the counters held dried fruit, flour, sugar, cereal

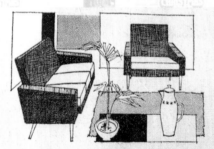

. . . AND your dividend if you buy from the NEWCASTLE

CO·OP

NEWGATE STREET

AVALON

products, pots and tins etc. Butter was a large block on a marble slab, bought loose, as were cheese and eggs. Loose foodstuffs were weighed with brass weights on a large scale then wrapped in greaseproof paper. Dried fruit, sugar and other goods were wrapped in brown, blue, purple coloured paper bags. When the purchase was completed the assistant put your money into a metal tube which in turn went into a holder. This then shot through the air above your head on a wire which arrived at the cashier. The change and cheque came back the same way. To us small children this was magic; it fascinated us and we never tired of watching it, it seemed out of this world to our lives which were modest and had little day to day variety.

When I was about seven or eight I was trusted to cross busy Stanhope Street and go to the Co-op alone. I was given the shopping list and the cheque number; soon I knew it by heart and she didn't need to write it down, I still remember it now, 68505, not bad for a 78 year old!

The town centre Co-op had a lovely Art Deco façade. My mother always bought shoes there and shirts for my father when supplies became more plentiful after the war. In my school days in Newcastle I used to shop at the Co-op too. It was the only way I could afford to buy new shoes and pay a small sum weekly. That was called a club, for a fairly large part of my pocket money I was able to get one through my mother as she was a store member. My pocket money would be 50p in modern money!

Many years later, when I was living in America, I took my first born James for a trip to Newcastle in 1967. We spent some time with my parents in Stone Street, where they were still living before being rehoused. Looking out of the window, I remarked that the neighbours seemed to be moving house. 'No' my mother said 'he works for the *steal* works'. Seeing my puzzlement she added 'everyone calls the Co-op the steal works, as so much stuff is stolen!' Literally from the back of a lorry as the saying goes. How true this was I don't know, I lived in another world, but it probably wasn't on the scale of my mother's fertile imagination. All of this taught us 'war' children the value of financial independence and now I still profit from the lessons in a very different world; with my still small budget I watch amused at the differences between my old world and that of my children and grandchildren and their very different ideas of economy !

Patricia Bensdorp-Clark

My nana's divvy number in Walker Co-op was 1098 (which we always said as ten, nine and eight). My mam's number at Newcastle was 60199.

Nana belonged to Walker TG and I remember numerous dinner dances my mam attended with her firstly in the facilities at Newgate Street and later in Murton House. It was always a good meal and as a child in the 50s and 60s, it was something of a luxury to have ladies in smart black and white to wait on me.

I loved Newgate Street 'Stores' (we always called the Co-op 'the Stores' as it was a plethora of shops and departments, some with separate entrances off St Andrew's Street, such as the butchery and pharmacy). There was a lift at each end of the building but I think one went higher than the other. I seem to remember the shoe department was downstairs along with the hardware. The ground floor had materials and wool and then led into a grocery section up a couple of steps. Upstairs was the Ladies Fashions and up again to furniture. I can't remember which floor the offices were on, but I do remember going to queue up for the divvy every half year. My mother always kept the little slips of blue from her purchases and I always knew what to expect! As a child the shop seemed so large and sprawling that I feared getting lost.

I remember the jewellery department moved to Murton House; for my 21st birthday present from my mam I got Ciro pearls earrings and a pearl ring from my great aunt, that building seemed a poor relation to the main store.

Anne Nelson

My earliest memories of shopping is going to the Co-op with my mum and ration book to do the weekly shop. Butter and lard were in a barrel shape and the amount she needed was cut out. Bacon was sliced fresh. Occasionally bacon bones (spare ribs) were available to make a stock for broth. I remember bananas coming into the country after the war and queuing up for ages for them. We were only allowed two of them per family.

June Marshall

PREVIOUS PAGE) A 60S ADVERT FOR FURNITURE. THIS PAGE) A RATHER UN-'PC' ADVERT FOR MENSWEAR.

WOOLWORTHS

Again not a 'local' brand but again a northern powerhouse (this time a Scouse one) of a certain period, good ol' Woolies had to get a mention…

Woolworths seemed to sell everything - make up, records, stuff for cleaning, toys, magazines and of course the famous pick n' mix.

Frank Woolworth imported his 'shop for all' concept from the US, his 'five and dime' model, changed for the British market so that everything was either 3d (1.5p) or 6d (2.5p). But he also imported the idea of bargains with 'class'. In 1909, his first store, in Liverpool, was opened 'for inspection only', and had two orchestras playing light classical music, with free pots of tea in the white table-clothed palm court restaurant. The next day, the crowds returned and the counters were practically stripped bare. By 1930, there were more than 350 stores nationwide.

On 17 December 2008, administrators announced that all 807 Woolworths stores would close with the loss of 27,000 jobs. People genuinely mourned the passing of such an iconic brand, something that was 'always there' – where now to get your pick n' mix? Well, Wilkinson's I suppose, as Wilco's could be the new Woolies!

Woolworths was perhaps jack of all trades, master of none – spreading itself too far – or perhaps it was just the victim of the financial crisis, and the huge increase in online shopping as other large companies such as BHS, Comet, MFI, Toys R Us and Maplin Electronics have also bitten the dust.

ABOVE) WOOLWORTHS ON NORTHUMBERLAND STREET, 1938. NEXT PAGE - TOP) THE 'REFRESHMENT' BAR IN TH_ NORTHUMBERLAND STREET BRANCH - HAM ROLLS, ASSORTED PIES, PASTIES AND PEAS ON THE MENU IN 193_ BOTTOM) WOOLWORTH'S ON GOSFORTH HIGH STREET, NOW A CO-OP, 193_

In 1960s Newcastle, I was eager to find a Saturday job; my parents were not well off and I wanted to contribute to the family income as well as having a little pocket money myself.

I braved the wrath of my PE teacher (who would have preferred me to continue turning out for the school hockey team) and began work in Woolworths on Northumberland Street. Assigned to 'haberdashery' I spent Saturdays in a wrap-around green nylon overall, selling ribbon, bra 'booster' inserts and a limited range of clothing. At that time, assistants had to ring for a supervisor if a customer tendered a five pound note - a lot of money in those days!

The days were often quiet and long, and I envied my friends working in the cafe, where it was all go. Eventually I obtained a transfer, and the hours now passed in a heated rush. The cafe consisted of a row of high stools facing counters along the east and south sides of the first floor. The 'business' side was a narrow strip between the ovens and the windows. Service was fast and furious, with a small lift at one end delivering food from the kitchen on the floor above, while at the other end a similar device whisked away dirty dishes and cutlery, replacing them with clean ones from the upstairs dishwashing machines.

During school holidays I often worked full weeks, and eventually I rose to the dizzy heights of 'Senior Saturday girl', earning a rise from fourteen shillings and fourpence to seventeen shillings and sevenpence.

Eventually the heat of the ovens got to me, and I found a cooler job with Bookless (fruit & veg) in the Grainger Market. I thoroughly enjoyed this change of scene. It was a friendly, busy community, and I liked setting up the displays, and chatting with the regular customers. Fruit and veg were very much more seasonal back then, and there was usually something different every week. I particularly remember the

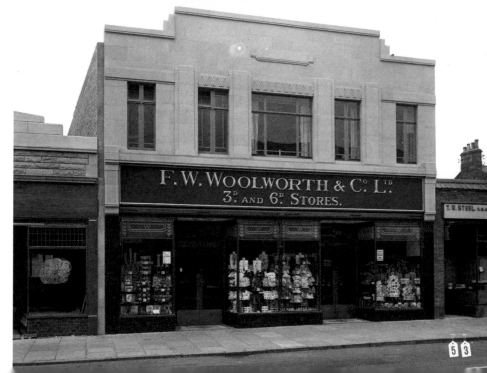

short bilberry season - they would arrive in large metal cans from Norway, and were often sold by the quarter pound (very carefully because of the juice which stained fingers and overalls).They were quite expensive; but our elderly customers eagerly anticipated baking their individual bilberry tarts on a saucer.

When I was at college in the early 1970s, the firm would regularly employ me during the holidays. I was often sent to other branches across Newcastle, but the Grainger Market remained my favourite. Considered to be a resourceful employee, I occasionally did the daily wholesale order and would be sent by the manageress to chase off the occasional mouse in the back shop.

Fifty years on, I enjoy shopping and have an eye for a bargain; however my experiences as a shop assistant mean that I am always polite to those who serve me - I have shared many of their experiences and worked those long hours too.

Linda Sutton

Although I worked in an office in Newcastle during the week, I worked in Woolworths on Clayton Street on a Saturday. My father had a men's hairdressing shop and I was lucky enough to have relatives with both fruit shops and grocery shops. This was in the late 40s and early 50s. I enjoyed working in retail and have great memories of Woolworths. My first memory was being told to get an overall from the cloakroom, some of which were new, but some had been already worn by other staff during the week! This wasn't a pleasant experience if a new overall wasn't available as the old ones could have been worn for weeks and the collars were ingrained with grease. So I made sure I arrived very early at work in order to find at best a fairly clean one. At Easter, gifts were made up in a huge room upstairs - baskets, fluffy chickens and sometimes chocolate eggs were made.

I worked on different counters but the one I especially remember was the grocery counter where jam, tinned foods, biscuits, etc. were sold. Cakes were also sold here, delivered in great slabs. Angel Cakes, Madeiras and a cake which consisted of three tiers - I think they were sold by weight after being cut to size. There were large tins with glass lids full of broken biscuits which we sold.

Towards the end of the day, the stock had to be replenished. Me and my friend had to go down the stairs, leading from a huge trapdoor in the floor behind a counter, to racks and racks of foodstuffs. The goods were packed into very large hampers which we had to carry and then negotiate up the stairs and onto the shop floor. How we did this I do not know, as they were packed full and hard to manage.

I also sold ice-creams which came in a large rectangular block and were encased in a light cardboard which you had to remove (our hands not to touch the ice-cream) and place from the container onto two wafer biscuits. If you were put onto the jewellery counter you were given strict instructions to watch customers' hands just in case they were tempted to take something without paying!

As my father had a shop, he only had half a day off during the week and this was Wednesday afternoon. I used to meet him at Fenwick's and he would take me to buy new shoes or clothes sometimes. There was a library and bureau in Fenwick's at that time and we used to go up there where he would choose books. He would then go to Smythe's cake shop near Fenwick's and buy a delicious cake for tea.

The town for me has always been special for shopping and I prefer it to the Metro Centre, which is far too closed in for my liking. In town you can stay inside the comfort of Eldon Square or go outside to other shopping locations, so Newcastle shops get my vote every time.

Anne Taylor

CLOCKWISE FROM TOP LEFT. 1) 1970S' NORTHUMBERLAND STREET. 2) VALUE! QUALITY!! SERVICE!!! – VEAL, HAM AND EGG PIE; FANCIES; BOVRIL AND 'DECKER' SANDWICHES ON THE MENU IN 1938. 3) 1984. 4) LOOKING DAPPER IN 1970.

MARCUS PRICE

The 1960s were shopping's heydey given that war time restrictions were long gone and a new youth fashion had exploded onto the scene, which placed you in one of two camps: the mods or the rockers. The rockers favoured Jackson the Tailor, but who was his 'mod' rival? Marcus Price of course...

My father opened the first Marcus Price shop in Blyth in 1929. In 1953 he managed to get a shop in Percy Street, Newcastle and that was the start of something a bit special. The 1950s was a very curious time. There were only three or four articles that seemed to sell: black trousers with turn ups, black and white salt-and-pepper tweed jackets, a few pullovers and an amazing range of shirts and ties. The window display probably featured 60 different shirts – every one boarded with stiff card pinned tightly. The ties were natty slim jims.

I remember the end of the flat cap. The guy that was selling them came into the Percy Street shop one day and my dad said, 'No, we're not taking any more,' pointing to piles of caps in the shop that just weren't selling, then he took the guy out into Percy Street. Dad asked him how many people were wearing caps – that's the acid test. There was no-one, yet 10 years earlier everyone wore a cap.

The 1960s arrived with a burst of energy and youth. I don't think any fashions since the 1960s caused so much of a culture shock. I suppose it reflected all the things that were going on in the world; political changes like the Civil Rights movement in the USA; a new sense of freedom; the fact that you didn't have to live with your parents and you had a bit more disposable income.

By 1960 I was running the Percy Street shop. We also had another shop in the Groat Market. It attracted more customers coming from places like Sunderland, Middlesbrough and Gateshead because their buses came into Worswick Street bus station and it was easier to reach from there. We were next to George Rye's shoe shop.

Bob Dylan bought a jacket and a tie in the Groat Market shop. I was working in Percy Street and the phone rang: 'Dylan's in!' That was in 1965. We were popular with other musicians too. Lulu used to come in and buy clothes for her band, The Lovers. She'd say 'he'll have that, that and that.' She obviously knew the look she wanted. The singer Billy Eckstine ordered two pairs of pants made to measure and we sent them to him in Hollywood Boulevard! The band leader at the Oxford would pick three ties and buy a dozen of each of them – whether they were for the band I don't know.

I was a jazz person – jazz was massive, but there was a lot of blues around too. Every big name seemed to come to Newcastle. I knew Alan Price well. One or two of us used to meet on Saturday lunchtimes in Pumphrey's. There was Alan Price, Nigel Stanger and John Walters who played with Alan Price (and later became a BBC producer – he produced John Peel).

We didn't cater for rockers, we dressed the mods. Jackson the Tailor was the place rockers went. Still, we did an awful lot of tailoring. Newcastle United footballers were a big part of trade. Our regulars included Frank Clark and Bryan 'Pop' Robson. We made Frank Clark's wedding suit.

As a shop we tried to be different – we didn't want anyone else in Newcastle to have the same lines. One of our best-sellers in the 1960s was the Ben Sherman shirt. The details like the pearl buttons and the hanging loop at the back were just right. We bought (and sold) so many that we were able to tell the manufacturer that we didn't want anyone else in Newcastle to sell them. Ben Sherman did a long version of the shirt which was a woman's knee-length frock. I remember a big rack in all the colours in the Percy Street Shop.

Another popular line in the 1960s was Levi jeans. Farnons was the only other shop in Newcastle to stock them. The Blyth shop stocked Levi's because they were a work jean and it was a working port – seamen could get them in New York and they wanted to get them in Blyth too. It was an industrial look. That was probably why we started stocking them in the Newcastle branches. Apparently the seamen used to hang them over the back of the ship and that bleached the colour and smoothed the fabric. Later the idea was taken up commercially and became known as salt washing. The problem with Levi's was that you couldn't get them all the time. The company claimed that the factories were supplying the US army in Vietnam and that was what caused the shortages.

Our typical customer was certainly young. We were never the cheapest clothes shop, but a lot of our customers were at art school. We were selling shirts at 21 shillings but the main shirt lines cost 27s 6d and some shirts sold for 32s 6d – that was a lot of money in the days when a girl working in C & A would earn £3 a week. I think things lasted a bit longer – fashions didn't change quite as quickly as they do now. Having said that, the Beatles jacket came and went fairly quickly. We did one in foam-backed fabric as well as one in leather. In the early 60s the price of a suit was £14, but then we imported an Italian suit with lined trousers that retailed at £27 10s. It was a huge price but we sold it. Then we saw the opportunity to move up-market was there and we started to import more stock. We would buy clothes from Holland and fly them into Newcastle but the paperwork was incredible.

We opened the Grey Street shop in 1967 as part of our move up-market. We were selling expensive articles from the beginning and stocked hand-made clothing and silks. When the average shirt cost between £1 10s and £2, the silk shirts in the Grey Street branch cost between £4 and £5. Normal ties cost between 8 and 10 shillings, but we charged 30 shillings for the pure silk ties in Grey Street. In fact the pure silk ties sold amazingly well and the manufacturers were astonished.

Other good sellers in the 1960s were three-buttoned, straight-fitting dark jackets with narrow lapels and muted stripes, Beatle-style collarless suits, flower power shirts and ties to match. We also sold those awful smelly afghans and leather vests. We were good on coats and raincoats. One of the lecturers in the University fine art department had a wife who made flowered ties. We bought them and they sold well. I went to Liberty's in London and bought yards and yards of their fabric. I had it made up into ties and we sold thousands. A lot of 1960s fashion was very dandyish, and of course anyone could wear a flowered tie to show how free and trendy they were.

Marcus Price

I managed Marcus Price's shop in the Groat Market all through the 1960s. You went past Pudding Chare and it was next to George Rye's shoe shop. It had a central entrance and a long window on each side of the door. Shirts were a big thing then. People always wanted shirts and ties. It was great fun!

We stocked ties in stripes and polka dots. Later, when flower power came, all the ties had to be in flowery material. We were going out and buying curtain material and remnants and so on and sending them away to our tie manufacturers. They were a load of rubbish! They wouldn't hang right. We sold flowery shirts too and then the more pretentious manufacturers used to do them in boxes with matching ties ... hideous. And then there were the hipster trousers made up in the most unlikely material, heavy tweeds in checks. We got into nicer quality merchandise eventually. It wasn't that long after post-war austerity in a way. Marcus knew people from the art school and the university. We saw a lot of students but they didn't seem to have as much money as students today. We were mostly selling to working-class lads who had money. City Stylish were our rivals, but they weren't much cheaper. Our Grey street shop was more up-market.

The best seller in the early 1960s was a strange and revolting pullover, knitted across ways with a batwing effect, with a basic body colour in red, black or mid blue and a stripe. It was called the Albatross. It sold very well, pre-Beatles. Before the Beatles came the scooter craze. The mod jacket was an Italian style, three button, short bum-freezer, usually in stripes, blue and grey, blue and black, brown and black and they sold like wildfire. Then there was the famous Beatle jacket with round neck and buttons, sometimes shiny, and piped edges.

In May 1965 Bob Dylan came into the shop with Alan Price and a couple of others, to buy clothes. He was very well-mannered and polite and was very taken with a traditional black blazer with shiny buttons which he bought, plus a pink shirt and multi-coloured tie. The teenage assistants were very excited, but didn't hassle him for an autograph.

David Bell, manager of Marcus Price, Groat Market

BOB DYLAN AT MARCUS PRICE CHOOSING A TIE.

Percy Street in the 1950s was an incredibly interesting part of Newcastle even though it was not a major part of the centre.

From the Haymarket to the Gallowgate turning, you had a series of small and extremely active businesses including the Pram Shop and Mark Toney (who are still in Percy Street today). Then the Levy brothers store and Steel's wool shop. There was a tool shop, known as the scissor shop because it had a massive pair of chrome automated scissors in the shop window. Next was Kiddy Kot, a children's clothes shop. Then on to the Pipe Hospital and the shellfish shop owned by a Mr Ephraim, who lived above the shop.

Across the road was a small terrace of old stone-built shops with a cobbled corner before the pavement. The one I remember was an antique shop belonging to a Mr Macdonald and his son. It became the new Barclay's Bank. Then there was the original Harker's ex-army store and Aynsley's, a building materials and hardware store. Between them and our shop was an animal skin business, which stank on a hot day in summer. Next to our shop was the record store belonging to Mr and Mrs Jeavons, this was excellent for popular music especially jazz and blues. After them was a Halford's and the famous bike shop Herby Ray's and lastly the Three Bulls' Heads pub. It was a very down-to-earth street.

The Percy Street shop was opened at Christmas 1953, and I joined it in January 1954 after two years in the army. The plan devised by my father was to have a shop catering to a youth market, say teens to twenties, because these customers were only catered for by one shop at the time, City Stylish.

A lot of fashion influences came from America: pop music, jazz, the blues, ice hockey, magazines such as *Esquire*, and of course record covers, especially ones by David Stone Martin.

The shop itself had a modern look; a shiny black glass fascia with our name in large sharp red neon lettering, at one side is the logo of a man in a tails and cloak with a top hat – the very opposite of what we were selling. Within this arcade we had a lot of widow space and it was the window dressing where we really made our mark.

Marcus Price

MARCUS PRICE
– Bridges the age gap

MONEY AND THE WAY WE SHOP

Remember the days before plastic? 'What!' you say, 'You mean we couldn't buy things on credit?' No, don't be daft, you could still buy things on credit, there were just different names and processes: times when tick and divvy meant different things and cheque books were all the rage. Remember when, heaven forbid, shopping was merely a necessity rather than a recreational activity; days when you went to buy clothes only when your last ones fell apart rather than as a social event or a mooch with your pals. How times have changed…

In my day men didn't seem to work in shops, it was always women serving you! If you wanted clothes they weren't available for you to select yourself, you had to ask the assistant. I'd go to the cheapest shop I could find and ask for a pair of knickers which the assistant would then pull out and I'd be able to make my selection from there. Many a time we would use tickets to buy goods, which had to be for the address shown on the ticket, which could cause problems given that these tickets were sold on or acquired elsewhere. On one such occasion I was using a ticket purchased elsewhere when my son kindly piped up to the shopkeeper that it wasn't our address. She must have been used to such misdemeanors though as she didn't bat an eyelid and the sale went through without question.

Nancy Davidson

Among the many shops on Stanhope Street was the Pawn Shop, close to the Post Office. My mother used to look in the window and admire the things for sale there. These were things not claimed by the owner who had borrowed money on their value. It was said to be a very profitable business as the loan was much less than the value. Mother had set her eyes on a pair of silver earrings with diamonds. They were very formal and not at all suited to her lifestyle but she remained a romantic at heart. I don't ever remember her wearing them, the diamonds were paste of course and the silver setting white metal. I still have them in my jewellery box and I too have never worn them, as some of the 'diamonds' are missing and they are rather heavy, but

they are precious to me as part of my mother's dream. The pawn system reminds me of the 'pay day' loans of today, with exorbitant interest rates for people who are desperate.

The pawn shop was much less extreme. My mother used to quote Shakespeare at me 'neither a borrower nor a lender be...' when I sometimes borrowed pennies from her during the week for sweets or some small trifle, to be paid back on Friday when father gave us our pocket money. Mother's purse was as safe as Fort Knox as far as 'foolish' spending was concerned. She had known poverty as a child in the First World War, her father was 'in the trenches'and her mother worked in a preserve factory in Gateshead.

The pawn system was used by many families in our neighbourhood and mother looked down on them. She found them feckless, especially one family where there were two sons and a father, all working. Their mother pawned their suits on Monday and reclaimed them on Saturday, so that they could be neatly dressed for the weekend pub ritual. The pawn money was part of her housekeeping money during the week. My mother never seemed to understand that lots of women couldn't cook or housekeep as well as she could and often had many more children than our family of four.

Patricia Bensdorp-Clark

I can remember getting a 'provident' for Marcus the Furrier (which is where Santander is now) for an Afghan coat. I also bought two pairs of loons from Marcus Price which someone stole off the washing line! I couldn't wait to make enough money to shop at C&A without needing 'tick' to get my clothes.

Francis Renforth

When I was little, in the late 1940s, clothes shopping was for a reason or a special occasion, it was never just a pastime as it is today. It was a necessity

CLOCKWISE FROM TOP LEFT. 1) HURRYING DOWN NORTHUMBERLAND STREET, EARLY 70S. 2) OUTSIDE MARCUS THE FURRIER AT THE JUNCTION OF NORTHUMBERLAND STREET AND NORTHUMBERLAND ROAD, EARLY 70S. 3) SELLING PAPERS OUTSIDE THE BEEHIVE PUB, BIGG MARKET. 4) SATURDAY SHOPPING IN THE GREEN MARKET.

not an amusement. No one was wasteful or threw clothes away until they were well worn out. If we grew out of them then they were passed on to someone else who was smaller. If they were no longer wearable then they were sold to the rag and bone man. He came around the streets with his horse and cart. My husband was from Throckley and insisted that the rag man had a trumpet to call out the householders. Sometimes he would give out a goldfish instead of money which wasn't popular with our mothers.

Elspeth Rutter

My nana lived on Kendal Street in Byker, she ran a 'diddlin club'; people paid her 6p a week for her to save for them until Christmas when she handed over the cash. Presumably she kept a commission! She was a widow with seven children (four had died) and took in the washing of rich people in Heaton so she had to use her ingenuity to make ends meet. She carried the washing in a basket on her head – how did we lose that skill?

Parrish's cheques were popular in Byker. People bought them with a Provident cheque, so it was in essence shopping on the tick! However, people who were really hard up would sell their £1 Parrish cheques (which were plastic coins) for 15/-. My aunties bought up the bargain coins but I being a righteous Catholic lass thought it was immoral to take advantage of poor people; though my aunties worked very hard and were not much above the poverty line themselves.

Olya Bower

My shopping habits have changed now. I shop more in supermarkets for my clothes and shoes etc. Something which was unheard of years ago. These days I pay for things on debit or credit cards but it used to be paid for by a Provident book of vouchers.

Denise Gibson

As a child in the sixties I was often sent to a local grocer at Lemington Road Ends with a shopping list – I usually had to ask for it to be 'put onto my mam's bill'. I used to earn 3d or 6d by getting groceries for neighbours as well. I remember the excitement in the late 60s and early 70s when the grocer closed and it was turned into a 'Chinese chip shop'. We only ever bought chips but they tasted so different from the ones we got from the chippy.

Sue Jeffs

In the 50s and 60s shopping was by cash only and a trip to town with my mum and grandma was a huge treat as a child. The shopping was followed by a trip to the Tatler cinema, which was not too frequent a trip as it was quite expensive. Now an outing to town and visit to the cinema are an accepted weekly or even daily occurrence due to the increase in disposable income. How times change!

Lorraine Harvey

The annual trip to the Wills factory on the Coast Road was always something to look forward to. Armed with a year's supply of Green Shield Stamp books (courtesy of the many petrol stations that used to supply them) the whole family would go to the reception area at the front of the building to hand over the stamps for counting. After having perused the catalogue for weeks in advance, we included our handwritten order of various household, kitchen and garden appliances and the odd toy or game (from the leftover stamps). It was always with baited breath that we waited for confirmation that all was in order and there were no gaps on the pages from 'escapee' stamps.

Simon Carey

A BUSY NORTHUMBERLAND STREET, 1950S.
RIGHT) METHODS OF SAVING AND PAYING - CO-OP STAMPS SAVING BOOK, EMBASSY CIGARETTE VOUCHERS, GREEN SHIELD
STAMPS, PARRISH'S TOKEN.

My mum got her groceries from the Co-op, she would take the order in on a Monday and they would deliver on a Thursday. I could never really understand why my mum would walk all the way to the shop and not bring stuff home – although we didn't have a car so it was probably easier. Imagine having to wait over two whole days for your shopping to arrive! Actually, don't, because it hasn't changed much - except that you order online now instead of in person. The only thing that *has* changed is the contents of the basket - what on earth did we do with four pounds of sugar a week?! I guess the answer is that we did our own baking and made our own jam. When sugar was rationed in 1974 (true kids - look it up!) we thought the world had come to an end!

We also had to get tokens for the milkman, who delivered bread too. During the other weekdays, there were regular visits by the fruit and veg man with his horse and cart, as well as eggs and fish delivered from the back of a van. Once or twice a 'genuine' French onion man even visited – complete with stripy shirt and bicycle, although he was probably more likely from Blaydon than Boulogne! The pop man came around with our regular order of a bottle of orange squash and a refill for my dad's soda syphon. If I remember, the syphon itself was 'on loan' and subject to a five shilling deposit. Pop bottles generally also had a few pennies' deposit, which was returned when you took back the empties. Many small children could supplement their pocket money by finding discarded ones by obviously wealthy persons who could afford to forego this revenue stream.

Some people collected Green Shield Stamps, mostly from petrol stations as I recall. We shopped at the Co-op, so we had dividend stamps. I remember my dad bought a set of ladders one day; it must have cost a lot, because we filled two books with the stamps he brought home with it. You could exchange them for discounts although we never collected enough to get anything really big; even the sum total of my dad's ladder purchase only amounted to a couple of pounds, which I think came off our grocery bill.

My grandad collected coupons from cigarettes. He must have got through a lot of fags as he had a drawer full. I remember flicking through the catalogue to see what could be purchased from this magnificent hoard, eyeing up the garden furniture you could get for several thousand ... unfortunately the total once more fell short as we had to settle for a hairbrush and mirror!

In the end, the stamps lost their appeal and were discontinued. The catalogues remained however and I believe Green Shield became Argos, while Littlewoods opened a series of Index stores with the same business model. 'Catalogue' shopping has become more popular, particular since it went online, with Amazon showing the way despite a shaky start. But for my part, you can't beat feeling and seeing the goods first, trying them on or tasting them – although our local sweet shop owner might have disagreed – but then he shouldn't have had them on display!

Roland Finch

Mr Allan, the butcher, was a grandfather like figure who was in cahoots with my mother during the Second World War. There were queues for meat in those days, tiny amounts per person per ration book. To my surprise my mother told me that all books had the same meat ration for child or adult. Luckily for father's appetite for meat, I didn't eat any for quite some time. I was born in March 1939, 'Hitler was coming' but I got there first.

One thing that was not rationed was sausage, the implication being you could make it with very little meat. Mothers were often in the sausage queue for hours, mine made life long

GREEN MARKET, 1970.

acquaintances there. In her seventies and eighties when we were shopping in town, she would bump into someone and have a chat: 'I met that girl in the sausage queue' she would say.

Mr Allan would now and then surreptitiously add a little extra something to mother's brown paper bag. A sheep's head for delicious broth, liver or hearts for stuffing. These things were not rationed but as he told my mother 'these young things today don't know how to cook them'.

Patricia Bensdorp-Clark

In the 60s one of the biggest changes in clothes shopping was the fact that we now had 'teenagers', a very new concept! There was also a bit more money around. As well as teenagers the word leisure was new. It wasn't only the rich who could ride horses, play golf and tennis or have time to pursue hobbies. Clothes for various leisure activities started to appear in the shops. I remember being asked to design cruise wear at college. Who went on cruises? Foreign package holidays were becoming available, and clothes for these were in the shops also. Young people had some money of their own in their pockets. They could buy themselves clothes on a whim and not from necessity.

When I was at Art College I decided that my mother's choice of clothes for me was not what I wanted. I 'needed' my clothes to be black or purple! I rebelled against the 'good coat from C&A' and discovered Harker's Army and Navy Store (beloved by Eric Burdon who was also at Art College) It was run by John and Peter Harker's mum. They would later open the denim world of Plus Four. Harker's was a treasure trove of clothes on high layers of rails. They had army surplus, American workwear, overalls, dungarees and jeans. Here I got my duffle coat. It was warm and cheap and I thought I was so cool. I was transformed into a beatnik with that one garment. At least I thought I was! By this time there was a little more choice of clothes in the shops in general. We had left the depravations of the war years behind us and there was now more disposable income. However it would be a while before the present day era of shopping as a pastime.

The idea of putting wearable clothes into a charity shop was also not heard of. Churches had jumble sales and worn out woollens and clothes were bought by dealers to be sold on. The cottons went to make paper among other things and the woollens were reused to make new woollen garments, carpets and insulation. With clothes shopping there was still room for independents, we had travelled from the 50s to early 60s (dressing the same as our mothers), to suddenly in the 70s wearing what we wanted. We needed to look different from our friends and peer group. As young people had more money they followed the different styles that they wanted; Punk, Hippy, Ethnic, Retro, Sloane Ranger, Classic, Laura Ashley romantic...! The world was our oyster, even in Newcastle and the department stores couldn't keep up. To keep pace with the changing fashions in 1975 our local Bainbridge's store (who was usually stocked by John Lewis central buying) had the

CLOCKWISE FROM TOP. 1) THE INTERIOR OF MARCUS PRICE, 1955. 2)WOOLWORTHS ON NORTHUMBERLAND STREET, 1955. 3)LOOKING FOR THE LATEST FASHIONS IN BOOTS, NORTHUMBERLAND STREET, 1970. 4)EVE BROWN, NORTHUMBERLAND STREET, 1956. 5)TEEN & TWENTY ROOM AT AMOS ATKINSON - RAVE FOOTWEAR FOR THE YOUNG SET?

foresight to allow local purchasing. They stocked jackets, skirts and dresses and blouses from Elle boutique in the Haymarket and put them in their new 'trend' department. Quickly the other big stores opened 'young' departments as well as their usual classic ranges. Sensibly, they remembered that the whole world was not populated by teenagers. This new teen market was very quick to change direction and clothing buyers had to be paying attention or the customers would be off, spending their money somewhere else.

Elspeth Rutter

In the early 70s I'd just started working for Newcastle Library Service and was earning relatively good wages. Based in the City Library I was very well placed to look around the shops during my lunch hour and decide which items of clothing I was going to buy on pay day. My usual technique was to 'put things away' and then spend my lunch hour on pay day rushing from shop to shop, picking up all my purchases and paying for them. I would then hurtle back to the library with minutes to spare, weighed down with carrier bags and with a large proportion of my monthly wage already spent! My favourite shop in the early 70s was Bus Stop - set in a Georgian building painted Pillar Box Red, it had a dark moody interior and clothes to die for. The materials were beautiful in themselves, crepe de chine, crushed & panne velvet, satin and silks. Garments often featured very detailed finishing such as piping & exquisite buttons and the fabrics often had a vintage feel, that tapped into the early 70s' trend for Art Deco.

The trend had been the trademark of famous London store, Biba. Favourite buys from that time included a suit from Bus Stop with a black background, featuring a bold pattern of Flamingos and Palm Trees. A jacket in turquoise panne velvet, a suit in chocolate crushed velvet & a beautiful blouse from the designer Jeff Banks (sold in Fenwick's) covered in hummingbirds . However, my all time favourite from that era, was another Fenwick's buy, a raspberry coloured crepe wrap over dress by the designer Ossie Clarke.

Kath Cassidy

ELDON SQUARE, HABITAT, 1982.

GANNIN' FER THE MESSAGES

Thuh'res certain words uz Geordies use, that need some clear translation,
That divvent really travel Sooth, withoot some education.
Some o' them are local, an' are nivvah heard elsewhere,
An' others are in language which the Scots fowk ahlso share.
'Ah'm gannin' fer the messages', ye divvent hear theday,
It means yuh're gannin' shoppin, in a very different way,
From the supermarket visit, where it's ahll stacked in one place,
Where yuh wander with yuh're trolley, an' yuh're just anotha face,
In a sterile shoppin' temple, where yuh meekly join the queue,
As yuh're processed through the check-oot, an' yuh pay the money due.
Hoo diff'rent from me Grandma's day, whee 'went along the top',
Wi' two 'message bags' shuh carried, as shuh wahlked from shop te shop.
Shuh did her shoppin' evr'y day, nee fridge or big chest freezer,
As shuh chatted te her neighbours, hoo those daily trips would please her.
Wi' 'Good mornin' Mrs. Conway, hoo's your Jimmy gettin' on?'
Shuh'd enjoy a reet good gossip on her message marathon.
From the Butcher te the Baker, with nee trolley there te push,
As shuh wandered roond the Co-op shuh was nivvah in a rush.
Shuh used her Divvy number as shuh settled up te pay,
As ah sometimes got those messages ah remember it teday.
Hadrian, MacFisheries, so many names lang gone,
Pushed oot by faceless shoppin' malls wuh noo depend upon,
As wuh make the weekly dash aroond, te fill that shoppin' trolley,
Ah knah it's more convenient, but it leaves wuh melancholy,
Compared te Grandma's 'messages', with time te hev a chat,
As shuh wandered on an' stopped te buy a bit o' this an' that.
An' yes, wuh've far more choice noo, an' it's easier te store,
Nee daily shop 'along the top' te get wuz oot the door.
Ah suppose wuh've made some progress, but it ahll comes at a cost,
An' though wuh shop until wuh drop, ah wonder what wuh've lost…

Michael McCarthy

STOPPING FOR A CHAT IN THE GRAINGER MARKET

CLOCKWISE FROM TOP LEFT: 1) LOWE AND MOORHOUSE AT THE JUNCTION OF NORTHUMBERLAND STREET AND BLACKETT STREET (1930). 2) OLD SHOPS ON PERCY STREET. 3) PEGGY MOORE AND HER GRANDDAUGHTER IN A TYPICAL CORNER SHOP IN SCOTSWOOD. 4) SINGER SEWING MACHINE SHOP AT THE JUNCTION OF NORTHUMBERLAND STREET AND ST MARY'S PLACE - NOW OCCUPIED BY TSB BANK.

CLOCKWISE FROM TOP LEFT: 1) A LARGE SELECTION OF CHINA IN L. MARTIN'S (1936) 2) R.W. BURRELL BUTCHER SHOP ON CHILLINGHAM ROAD (1949). 3) QUEUING OUTSIDE ROWLAND BLAYCOCK ON NEW BRIDGE STREET - THE SIGN IN THE WINDOW SAYS 'QUEUE HERE FOR LADIES HOSIERY DEPARTMENT' (1950).

REGIONAL SHOPPING

Although Newcastle city centre has always arguably been the region's main shopping location, there has always been the need for more local shopping too; particularly given that cars were few and far between in the not so distant past and travel arrangements were an additional cost that poor folk simply could not at times afford. Step forward the saviours of regional shopping; those out of town department stores or even just local corner shopkeepers who would keep families ticking along (sometimes on tick) without the need to venture far…

EAST END

I borrowed a wedding dress and veil and my mother bought my wedding suit in the ladies' toilets of the Butcher's Arms! It was pink nylon and horrible but it was cheap! Window shopping was a social occasion and Shields Road was great for this because of the wide pavements. You'd walk along there arm in arm with your mother or your pals and comment on the arrangements in windows, style of dresses, prices etc. It was good, free, fun but these days you are faced with metal shutters on Shields Road and it has become lifeless after dark.

Olya Bower

My story is a recollection of staying with my grandmother in Byker during the war, in her little two up, two down terraced house. I was about nine and my sister Sadie ten years old, so 1942 or thereabouts. Before the days of indoor plumbing, with the netty or earth closet in the back yard, chamber pots were of course a bedroom necessity. Freshly emptied and washed, my grandmother had left the pot on the bottom step one morning ready to be taken back to the bedroom when next she went upstairs. My sister, not realising it was there, came jumping down stairs two at a time and broke the china pot. Disaster! So Sadie and I were sent out to find an urgent replacement. We walked for what seemed like miles around Byker, Heaton, along Shields Road and Chillingham Road, trying to find a hardware shop that had a chamber pot for sale. Nobody had one. And we couldn't return home empty handed - the chamber pot was essential. We had started to give up hope when we happened upon a corner shop - it could have been a perfect replica of Ronnie Barker's Arkwright's *Open All Hours* store. I wish I could remember the name of the street, but it is one of those long since demolished and replaced by the Byker Wall estate. Anyway, by good luck the elderly shopkeeper had a pot which we gratefully bought, but he had no spare paper in which to wrap said item. So, with much embarrassment my sister and I set off home to grandmother's carrying the china chamber pot in full view for all to see. But do you know, we were stopped by so many people asking where we had bought the pot as they too had been unable to find one. So we happily gave directions. I'm not sure what the bemused shopkeeper must have thought because he would have sold many chamber pots on that day as we kept directing people to his store. It's funny that of all the wartime memories of staying with my grandmother, it's not the tin air raid shelters, or the open bomb sites where we played, but this memory of carrying a chamber pot through the streets of Byker and being stopped by grown-ups, all anxious to know where they too could buy one, that sticks in my mind!

Sheila Lloyd

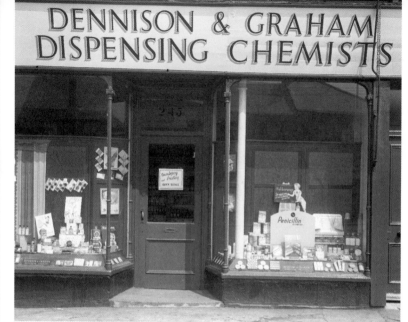

When I was young we used to live above a butcher's shop. Mother used to make the pies every morning, and occasionally when I was off school I was allowed to help. I loved watching her with the very heavy pastry press that she used to line the pie tins, then she added the filling, on the top she used the same pastry press but with a different fitting which would seal the pies. I was then allowed to paint the pies with an egg wash. I loved it when they came out of the oven as I was always allowed to have one served with a very generous dollop of HP sauce. My favourite was the pork pie, mmm, my mouth waters at the thought of them now. Mrs Ball, the butcher's wife, always made a cup of coffee to go with the pies but it was made with 'Camp' coffee which at the time I loved as she laced it with sugar. These days I cannot imagine what I would think of it as it was made with chicory. The queues used to be out of the door when the pies were due out the oven.

The bags of flour were stored in a cupboard under the stairs and quite often you could see weevils crawling around in the flour bags. Mr Ball, the butcher, used to sieve the flour to get rid of them.

Sawdust was thrown on the floor to catch the drips of blood from the carcasses hanging up. This made it easier to clear up at night as they just used to sweep the sawdust up then scrub the butcher's block.

They used to have a Christmas Club where people were given a little card and each week Mr or Mrs Ball would mark on it how much the customer had paid, it soon mounted up and by Christmas you had enough cash it in to buy your turkey (it used to be a large chicken in our house!), sausages, bacon, and other meats. The newsagent was where Santa bought most of our toys from - as we used to get a catalogue in the summer to browse through so you had an idea what you wanted.

Shawn Fairless

I remember two little shops at the top of our street in Walker. One was a typical old sweet shop and one selling veg. My aunt worked at Hornby's Grocers shop on Station Road, Walker which was a few streets away from our house; when we moved to Benton, Mam would give them a weekly order for store cupboard items such as flour, sugar, butter, biscuits and tinned items.

Young Mr Hornby would arrive in his little van on a Saturday morning with the order in a box; such great excitement to see what was in the brown paper bags, which usually had the prices marked on them in pounds, shillings and pence. I can remember him always wearing a brown overall coat and a pencil behind his ear; he only came for a few months as new shops were starting to open in Benton. Eggs were bought when we visited grandparents in Byker from J Lowrie's egg merchants on Brinkburn Street; again these were put into brown paper bags so you had to be very careful when carrying them. Fresh bread on a Saturday was again bought in Byker from Fairbairns on Raby Street, always a couple of flat cakes which was a bit like a stottie. Fresh veg and fruit came from Sarah's hand cart on Shields Road; she was there all weathers and recognised us so my brother and I always got handed a 'try this satsuma or strawberry' depending on the season. There were heavy bags to carry onto the bus to take us to Benton! I loved going to Shields Road on a Saturday though as it meant a trip to Woolworths for a pick and mix to eat on Saturday night whilst watching TV. If we had been really good there was a trip to Mark Tony's at the bottom of Shields Road for an ice cream floater. Mam would then go and look in Marika's across the road which stocked high class clothing and hats. Looking is all we ever did unless there was a wedding in the family, then she would treat herself to a pair of fine gauze stockings.

Pat Rogerson

CATCHING UP WITH THE
NEIGHBOURS? SHIELDS
ROAD, 1972.

WEST END

I walked for miles down Elswick Road to a shop that had Pontefract cakes with coconut on them. I got them and put the coupons back in my handbag. On the way home I realised that I had left the bag in the shop. I went back about ten minutes later and the bag was gone, with all the sweet coupons – two pages of them that were meant to last for a whole year. I was KILLED when I got in. I came home with nothing apart from the sweets I had in my mouth!

Mary McArdle

I used to live in the Benwell Terraces and my grandma lived in the next street. She'd often take me shopping on Adelaide Terrace, but I found it REALLY boring. When you think back to how many shops you'd have to go in to just get simple groceries - the butcher, the baker, the fruit shop, the chemist - now of course it's all under one roof. She'd drag me down there - pulling that shopping cart all old ladies seemed to have back then and we seemed to visit every shop where she'd chat forever to the shopkeeper. At the end of what seemed like hours of shopping, with my legs tired and my feet feeling like they were about to drop off - what was my treat? Straight past the sweet shop and into the bakers where I was given a plain bread bun! When we eventually got home I loved helping put everything away because I'd get the collectable card from the box of PG Tips.

David Archibald

PREVIOUS PAGE) ADELAIDE TERRACE, 1970. TOP) A TROLLEY BUS ON ADELAIDE TERRACE, 1960. RIGHT) PULLING THE SHOPPER ALONG ADELAIDE TERRACE, 1990.

GOSFORTH & JESMOND

Rationing was taken off sweets later than some of the other commodities. My sister and I were allowed to go on our own to the sweet shop on Station Bank in South Gosforth, with 3d each. All the local children queued there to buy sweets. For food shopping we got an order once a week from Wilkinson's the grocer on the High Street in Gosforth. It was delivered by a boy on a bike with a big basket at the front. We went down to the shops for anything not on the list. We got our bread from Robson & Porteus beside the Brandling Pub, they baked on the premises and I loved waiting in the queue smelling the lovely aroma of freshly baked bread. They were one of the rare places that had brown bread which was my mother's favourite.

Wilkinson's the grocers was a large shop and compared to shops today it was quite dark inside. I think this was probably to keep stock cool. It had an open area in the centre with dark wooden counters round the edges. There was high wooden shelving on the walls behind the counters. At the back of the shop on the right was the bacon slicing machine and you were always asked what thickness you wanted your bacon cut. Also at the back were big rounds of butter on marble slabs this was cut and weighed as required. The assistant would use two ridged wooden paddles to handle the butter and it was wrapped in greaseproof paper. The sugar was kept in a wooden barrel and was weighed out and poured into blue paper sugar bags. When we went down to the shops for something my mother needed we usually went on our bikes. Me being a dippy child I would park my bike outside the shop and then forget it was there and walk home! Often I would rush back to the High Street and the bike was still there outside the shop. I don't think this would happen now!

Elspeth Rutter

Shops and shopping colour many memories. Especially from early childhood. I have vivid memories of Mr Johnson's sweet shop on the way to Jesmond picture house on Saturday afternoons for the kids' show - farthing chews, four for a penny, barley sugar twists, tiny plastic cups full of sweet candy with a tiny spoon. The thrill of having three pence or sixpence to spend. No wonder I had bad teeth!

As a small child growing up in Jesmond in the 1950s, I would walk daily with my mother to the local shops on St George's Terrace. First we would visit William White the grocer, where you bought biscuits from a big square tin box by weight - Custard Creams, Nice, Digestives. The till was huge, silvery, embossed with a swirling pattern, and made a satisfying 'kerching' as the lady (or maybe even Mr White) behind the counter pressed the keys. Everything was weighed out for you and placed in your basket. Then we might go round the corner to Brydon's fish shop for some fish tails for the cat, which was wrapped in newspaper. We sometimes walked down to the far end of the terrace to go to Leathard's the deli (only we didn't call it that), to buy maybe some cheese.

There was a better greengrocer at that end of the terrace, so much so that you had to queue up to be served. This was Barnet's, where Mr Barnet and his sons held court. I remember a board outside which always read 'Eggs are Cheaper' and we would always ask, cheaper than what? We might turn into Acorn Road and go down to Charlie's the butcher (well that's what we called the shop) where there was sawdust on the floor, carcasses hanging from hooks and chops wrapped in newspaper. Then on to the electrician who sold wirelesses and batteries as well as fixing things.

There was a toy shop on that street. I yearned for a clockwork monkey that played the drums and he turned up in my Christmas stocking, much to my delight. Shopping was a pleasure to me then; my mother usually met people she knew for a chat as we went and she knew all the shopkeepers too.

Annabel Flowers

**POSTCARDS OF
GOSFORTH HIGH STREET
FROM 1905.**

GROWING UP ON PERCY STREET

I was born into a local family – well sort of, just before 1950. My grandparents escaped the pogroms and harsh conditions on the Russian/Polish border at the start of the 20th century. They settled in Merthyr Tydfil where they were married at the local synagogue and, unable to find any work other than mining, my grandparents moved to Newcastle in around 1905 on the advice of friends from back home already settled up here. My grandfather established what eventually became a successful clothing and tailoring business employing around 60 people at its peak, but the second world war put pay to all that as it did to many others. My father, however, decided that wasn't for him and in 1935, having already established trading posts around the North East, decided Newcastle city centre – the Metropolis – was the place to be.

He was astute, and in those days as today, footfall and an economic price were the major deciding factors in choosing a location. The one street that predominated was Percy Street – the gateway into the city from the Haymarket Bus Station. Northumberland Street, even in those days was still out of his price range, and better still the more reasonably priced Percy Street was without a jewellery and watchmakers' shop.

My earliest memorable visits were with my grandmother who lived at the family home, Cavendish Place in Jesmond. She was a true matriarch, who loved nothing better than to prepare lunch then get the bus on Osborne Road with the meal in a wicker basket on one hand and me on the other, and off to town we would go. My father Lewis (Lewie) had been joined in the business by his two brothers Emmanuel (Manny) and Nathan (Natie). Once in town we soon arrived at the door of N.

& L. Fagleman Ltd, 36-38 Percy Street, and as soon as I walked through the door I knew I was home. To have a wonderful father was one thing, but to be blessed with two equally lovely uncles was a true bonus. There was no better place in the world.

Percy Street in my early years in the 1950s became my second home. It was more a little village than a street – in fact it was my own little world. Our family shop was located around midway on the east side, further down from Handyside Arcade.

My father's shop was of decent size and quite long. It was seldom empty. To the right of my father's shop, going towards the Haymarket was first of all Maynard's, where I experienced my first taste sensation of the 1950s – a packet of Tudor Cheese and Onion crisps – the second best invention after the wheel! Then there was Teare's, an antique and fancy goods shop, after that was Swinden's the cutler's with a gigantic pair of scissors, which sometimes moved with the aid of an electric motor, in the window. Next was Thompson's the Pork Butchers, and a fish and chip shop with red shutter (the smell of the old dripping was quite vile). Nearby was Grainger Boot Stores, where I begged my father to buy me a pair of winklepickers only to end up with the usual boring Oxford or Tuf shoes. Then there was Wright's, a drapery store that went round the corner ending up close to Bainbridge Hall, then round again to Prudhoe Street Mission and of course our local Co-op, where I had to give our 'Divvy' number and later get dividend stamps to stick in a little booklet.

The other way along Percy Street, heading south, was our neighbour the Pipe Hospital run by Chris McNeil. Around the corner in Eldon Lane was the 'Button King' run by the Adler family, upstairs from the Pipe Hospital. Across the lane was of course the Mecca for all children – Boydells, toy shop extraordinaire. The hours I must have spent staring in the window at all those Airfix kits and eagerly awaiting all the new Dinky and Matchbox vehicles to be on display. They never ceased to enthral me – what a shame I never kept hold of them in their original boxes, which of course went the journey not long after the day of purchase – if only we could read the future.

On the corner of Eldon Lane, just yards from our shop, was the lovely Liza Sayers who had a barrow selling fruit, six days a week whatever the weather. She had four sons, Frankie, John, Peter and Albert and a daughter called Sylvia, a bonny young lady who worked with her. Our family were very fond of them and my father was always compassionate towards her, as he knew she worked hard to support a large family. She sat by her barrow on a little stool with a small stove for boiling a kettle, which we always kept full. Nothing was taken for granted, any help she needed was on hand, and she always generously reciprocated with a nice melon or pineapple – luxuries in those days. I struck an immediate bond with her youngest, Albert, who was the same age as me. We stood on that street corner for many years – there was always plenty to chat about as well as a ready supply of fresh fruit, and that fruitful friendship has endured more than 50 years. My other buddies from those days still remain close friends – Terry Milligan who lived in St Thomas Street, and Peter Harker, whose father owned Harker's Army Surplus Stores across the road on the corner of Percy Street and Leazes Park Road.

Back on Percy Street, after Boydell's was Connor's – a boot and shoe shop where my father took me in 1959 to buy a pair of hob nailed football boots and a tin of dubbin, prior to my starting Heaton Grammar school. Next door was Onion's, a shop that sold animal food, mainly for dogs. At the rear of the

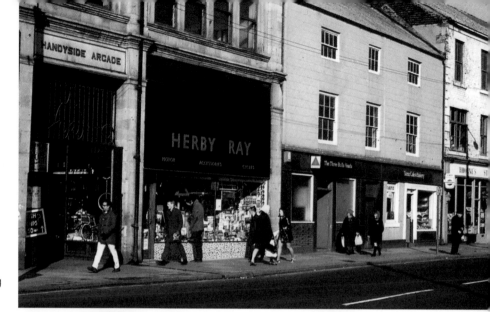

shop was an assortment of offal, off cuts and raw offerings scattered over the floor – tinned dog and cat food was not such a bad idea! Next to that was the next most odourful shop – Milburn's Shellfish Bar – a definite no-no to walk past on a hot summer's day before the bins were emptied. Next was Berry's, a small confectioner and tobacconist and then Prudhoe Court. After that was a small parade of shops, called Greig's, selling all sorts of clothing and drapery – almost Percy Street's answer to Harrods. Then came the local pub, the King's Head, where a little old newspaper vendor stood outside with his one leg and a crutch; we always bought our 3d *Evening Chronicle* from him. Crossing over Blackett Street, the shop on the corner was Milburn's, a pharmacy and also a bit of an apothecary's, much to the delight of my uncle Manny who was becoming a hypochondriac. I'll never forget the regular visits, particularly the one on which he acquired a bottle of Cascara Evacuant for suspected constipation. An over generous quantity of the recommended dose was taken and uncle was totally incapacitated for the rest of the week! Thereafter a cursory glance at the rogue bottle was an instant cure for the problem.

Back to the shop, I could go up and down the other side but one establishment 'out smells' all others. Waggott's Sheepskin Curing Warehouse was a true stinker, even more so because it was immediately opposite our shop. Daily wagons of sheep carcases, loaded up to the top and often overhanging, would drive up to the premises with its wide entrance and disappear inside. On a hot busy day the stench was so pungent that no one could pass by the premises – you had to cross over the road and give them a wide berth. Nevertheless, this was all part of the rich tapestry of Percy Street. Towards the end of the following decade it rose out of the ashes like a phoenix – the old warehouses and offices of the Handyside Arcade became the 'Carnaby Street' of Newcastle. I opened my first business there. God bless Percy Street.

Brian Fagleman

LOOKING NORTH ALONG PERCY STREET, C1900.

83

WOR CORNAH SHOP

Lang before them supermarkets came upon the scene,
Wuh did wor shoppin' locally, it woz part o' wor routine,
Te buy stuff ahlmost daily, an' wor much-repeated stop,
Woz the ahlwus open doorway o' wor well-loved cornah shop.
It woz quite a social centre, where neighbours met te chat,
As thuh went there fer thuh're 'messages'… a bit o' this an' that.
An Aladdin's cave o' goodies, such a range o' stuff te stack,
An' if yuh divvent see it there, it's mebbees oot the back..
Ah've such distinctive mem'ries, so quick te re-awaken,
A mixed aroma in the air, o' coffee, cheese an' bacon.
A geet big slab o' butter… thuh cut it wi' a wire,
An' stacked there in the cornah, wood kindlin' fer the fire.
Sugar from a barrel, scooped intah paper bags o' blue,
Boxes full o' broken biscuits, loose tea te mek yuh're brew.
Mistah Brodie took such pride in it, yuh could often hear him boast,
That he stocked the widest range o' goods alang wor north-east coast.
If yuh needed summat special, then yuh had a word wi' him,
As he saw it as a challenge, an' would ahlwus gerrit in.
As a bairn ah used te gan there, ah could think o' nee-where nicer,

Ah'd a fatal fascination wi' that scary bacon-slicer.
Ah can hear it noo, that swish 'n cut, wi' such un-errin' aim,
Stacked on greaseproof paper, wi' ev'ry slice the same.
Tinned goods were ahll the rage then. Ah can see them on display.
Carnation Milk, Bird's Custard, such a colourful array,
Wi' Spam an' tins o' corned beef next te sardines an' tinned fruit,
Cereals an' powdered milk, cordials te dilute.
Weekend Assortment, Wagon Wheels, a box o' Sherbert dabs,
Senior Service, Capstan, an' many othah tabs.
Ah bought me forst Woodbines from there, as then wuh knew nee
       better,
An' adverts described smokin' as a glamorous trend-setter.
Ah knah these days the supermarkets offer such a lot,
Wi' goods from ahll aroond the world, thuh'res so much choice
       wuh've got,
As wuh belt roond on wor trolley dash, an' stand there in the queue,
Faceless lines o'customers, wuh're quickly processed through.
So aye, thuh'res mair available, an' wuh shop until wuh drop,
But ah still remember fondly Mistah Brodie's cornah shop…

Michael McCarthy

OUTSIDE CLOUGH'S SWEET SHOP, HEATON, LATE 70S.

SHOPPING AS A NECESSITY

Sometimes it's not just food shopping that is a necessity! There are those events that occur throughout our lives or seasonal transitions which mean we have to pop to the shops for new items, like it or not…

BACK TO SCHOOL

Unless you were exceptionally good at playing hooky you had to go to school and if you had to go to school, you had to have a uniform, and if you had to have a uniform you had to go shopping for it…!

I remember the once a year trip to Isaac Walton to get a new school uniform. We were in awe of the big store with its dark wood and glass display cabinets, shelving and the superior assistants who thought they were so important. They would measure us with their tape measure even though my mother had already done this at home. As far as they were concerned the assistant was in charge. The uniform was of course purchased in a larger size so that I would grow into it. We sometimes bought a second hand uniform passed down to me but we still had to buy some bits and bobs from Isaac Walton. There was no stigma in this, it was practical and common sense. Shortages and doing without during the war were not a too distant memory.

Elspeth Rutter

In 1955 we would buy school uniform from Isaac Walton in Grainger Street or Raymond Barnes below the Theatre Royal. Shoes were from the Co-op: an order form was generated locally then we went to the main warehouse which is now the Discovery Museum. I remember the distinctive smell of fresh leather and the skill with which the shoebox was wrapped with brown paper, with sharp creases, tied up with string and how these 'experts' finished off the presentation with a carefully tied string carrying loop.

Ian Holloway

I got my school uniform from Isaac Walton. It was very expensive for uniforms back then, but I was given a government grant to help buy it – plus the school ran a jumble sale to sell used uniforms.

Olya Bower

I often visited Isaac Walton, who specialised in gentlemen's clothing, particularly sportswear, country attire and school uniforms. This was a far less pleasurable shopping experience. At that time it was situated next to the Grainger Market on Grainger Street. My Dad had an account there and being very traditional in matters of dress, he always bought his tweed sports jackets and overcoats from them. We kids got all our school shoes and school uniforms there. Despite its proximity, the environment was a million miles away from the hustle and bustle of the market. The atmosphere was hushed and reverential; we all started speaking in whispers as soon as we went in. The interior smelled strongly of polish, had thick carpets and was furnished with old fashioned cabinetry, made of glass, highly burnished brown wood and shining brass handles. As a child, my overriding impression of the place was that it was old fashioned, brown, dark and dingy. As one of the region's main

FORM AN ORDERLY QUEUE - OUTSIDE ISAAC WALTON, 1948.

suppliers of school uniforms, the colours of the clothes; predominantly bottle green, navy blue, brown and maroon, seemed to add to the sombre feel of the place. One of the most memorable things about the store was the docket system that was used to send information and payment from one department to another. This consisted of small leather tubes that flew around the store on metal rails situated behind the counters. I remember that I was fascinated by this and used to love watching them whizzing past.

Kath Cassidy

Wenger's was a medium sized department store where all of my school clothing was bought. This usually involved a last minute dash on the last Saturday of August to kit me out in the latest 'fashionable' uniform; along with many others who had also left it late. I detested trying on the different styles and sizes of trousers and blazers in the extremely basic and often cramped changing rooms; worse still was stepping outside where my mother would parade me catwalk-style in front of the other kids waiting to go in.

Simon Carey

WENGER'S DECORATED FOR THE KING'S JUBILEE IN 1935.

PILES OF COMICS FOR SALE AT 2D EACH AT WOOLWORTHS, NORTHUMBERLAND STREET, 1936.

Our school uniform consisted of: a tunic, blouse and tie; two pairs of knee high socks and two pairs of white ankle socks for summer; a felt hat; a panama hat; a blazer; cardigan; navy raincoat and of course two pairs of navy knickers with a pocket in for your handkerchief. We wore these for the gym with a white aertex shirt and black plimsolls. In the summer there was a pale blue summer dress with cream collar and cuffs; my mother usually made these although she didn't enjoy sewing. As we moved up the school we needed canvas hockey boots and gym shorts. For shoes we had a pair of lace ups and wellies and a pair of sandals for the summer. I don't know if the shoes were from Isaac Walton's, Binn's, Bainbridge's or Fenwick's, but I do remember the big x-ray machine in the shoe department as it was bigger than we were!

Elspeth Rutter

A BUSY MARKS AND SPENCER'S, 1983.

CHRISTMAS SHOPPING

If you are not a born shopper you can generally escape it for most of the year - until one particular time of year strikes: Christmas. Love it or hate it, Christmas shopping is a necessity for most and brings its own set of memories, customs and traditions. After all, you couldn't have a book about shopping in Tyneside without mentioning the tradition that is Fenwick's Christmas Window…

In December 1947, I was taken by my parents to the Fenwick's Christmas Toy Fair to see Santa Claus. I felt nervous for the first time but also excited. I even remember the clothes I was wearing! A new warm winter coat in a popular unisex design (boys wore blue, girls wore pink) and 'pullups' which were close fitting unisex trousers fastened at the sides with buttons or press studs. I still enjoy the Christmas Toy Fair and window display, which came later, at Fenwick's. I remember Christmas Shopping in Northumberland Street with crowds spilling out of the shops onto the Great North Road.

Ian Holloway

I remember Callers Christmas window way before Fenwick's. It was the first time I had seen little twinkling Christmas lights! Their Christmas windows were quite something!

Patricia Ward Lynn

We used to put money aside in the sweet shop on Shields Road for six months of the year in order to buy the kids chocolate at Christmas time. You always had to save up as you couldn't afford Christmas otherwise.

Nancy Davidson

I remember going to Shepherd's of Gateshead as a child, around the early 1970s, at Christmas. We sat in what was supposed to be a train taking us to Santa's grotto. There must have been some sort of conveyer belt device behind the fake windows so it looked like we were moving. As a five or six year old I really believed we were travelling somewhere magical, beyond the Gateshead store, until it was pointed out by my older sister that we had only exited by a different door. I then remember walking through fake trees with fairy lights until we reached Santa and his elves. After getting a gift, we then made our way back to the 'train' and back to shopping. Magical times!

Judith Newman

Fenwick's Christmas window always has and always will be a family tradition, I loved it as a kid and now love taking my children and watching their faces light up too. This is always accompanied of course with a trip to their fabulous toy department… though I'm sure this was bigger when I was their age!

Caroline McLaughlin

Fenwick's at Christmas was amazing and we'd visit Santa. Of course Fenwick's Santa was the real one, ones in the other shops were only helpers dressed up!

Diane Phipps

CLOCKWISE FROM TOP LEFT. 1) A DARK NORTHUMBERLAND STREET, FULL OF CHRISTMAS EXCITEMENT. 2) A SMALL CHRISTMAS FAIR ON NORTHUMBERLAND STREET, EARLY 90S. 3) THE REAL SANTA? AT PARRISH'S, 1950S. 4) AN ADVERT FOR THE CO-OP'S TOY FAIR AND 'NURSERY RHYMES' GROTTO.

FOOD

We all have to eat and unless we are part of a *The Good Life* style project, that means we all have to shop for our food...

A special occasion food shop was Smythe's, a local upmarket cake shop, bakers and confectioners. It had several branches in various suburbs. The city centre branch was situated on Saville Place. All the shops had the same interior decoration, featuring light oak panelling and gilt chandeliers. The assistants wore spotless white coats, hats and even put on white gloves when handling cakes. The smell inside the shops was divine. They also specialised in marzipan fancies in the shape of various animals. I remember we always visited to buy cakes for special occasions such as Christmas or Easter and my Mum always bought cheese straws from there if she was having a party. My Dad adored their Russian cake & I was particularly fond of the Pineapple Swiss Roll. It was a sad day when the owner retired and all the stores closed down.

I loved visiting Marks and Spencer's food hall which was renowned for its range and quality. At that time, local shops and the early supermarkets stocked fairly ordinary fare and didn't carry the range they do now. Marks and Spencer's was where you went if you wanted more exotic food for a party or special occasion.

Kath Cassidy

Once I was married, we tended to 'food shop' in the Grainger Market, where goods were always reasonably priced, good quality and very fresh! Yes you had to hump them home from town on the bus, but cost and quality were important. Supermarkets that sold everything were new in the 70s; it was an idea from the USA and as a result, high street shops such as bakers, butchers, fishmongers, grocers and greengrocers were starting to struggle. It was much easier to go to a big supermarket with a car park once a week and do 'one-stop shopping', than it was to trot around the different shops on the local high street with your shopping basket and lug it all back home twice or thrice a week.

After the war years, stock and variety of food in the shops became more abundant, giving us much more choice. We had always had lamb and butter from New Zealand, flour and tinned meat from America, bananas and sugar from the Caribbean and tea from India, but now specialities from Europe appeared: French cheeses, Spanish meats and onions, German sausages, Dutch cheeses, Italian pastas, tinned anchovies and sardines. Wine (for special occasions) from France, Italy, Spain and Germany. Who can forget Mateus Rose from Portugal? Foreign holidays were introducing us to these exotic delicacies; however we still didn't throw good food away or buy ready-made meals. Pork pies and fish and chips were ready meals then! There were no 'sell by' or 'use by' dates; even with a once a week shop our own common sense told us to use food in rotation and eat the more perishable goods first. The days of abundance and waste were still a long way off.

Elspeth Rutter

Sometime in 1950 we were heading through the Central Station from the 'Electric Platforms' towards the Main Line station when my parents spotted a pineapple in the kiosk (Finlays?) opposite Smith's Bookstall. It was the first pineapple they had seen since the start of WW2 and the first one I had ever seen. I knew a description of the pineapple but I had conjured up an image of a yellow 'hedgehog' rather than the shape of the real thing.

Ian Holloway

LEFT) MARKS AND SPENCER'S FOOD HALL, NORTHUMBERLAND STREET, 1986.

DICKMAN'S PIES

Who doesn't love a good pie? In the North East we are known for Greggs and the delights of a Sausage Roll or Corned Beef Pasty run deep. However, there was once another star baker on the pie scene: the infamous Dickman's Pies were made in a bakery on Pitt Street behind St James's Park and delivered to pubs and ravenous ship workers across the region.

These simple recipes made for working class Geordies were made using the best meat imported from Argentina: long before Coloccini and Guttierez became the region's most famous Argentine imports. With such close proximity to the hallowed Gallowgate, match days were particularly busy with queues of supporters lined up to get their favourite footie foodie fix: a humble pie. Offering great value for money the shop was always busy and match days particularly so.

A cry of 'the pies are here!' would follow deliveries

DICKMAN'S PIES ADVERTISED BEHIND THE BAR.

to Wallsend shipyards, generating a mass downing of tools as hungry dockers snatched goods from a large tray, all paid for in advance.

Mr Dickman had experienced a tough childhood but owning a successful business meant he now had something he could give back; leading him to develop a philanthropic attitude to those less fortunate. His motto was 'never turn a poor person away' and employees were encouraged to hand out misshaped goods from the back of the store to those in need: if none were left a piece should be broken from a 'perfect pie' instead so that no one went hungry.

The bakery produced many goods to satisfy a large local population. Breads included Edinburgh Brown, brown malt and white loaves. Cakes included fruit slabs and others with ingredients of raspberry, orange, ginger and coconut. There were jam and lemon tarts, ginger snaps, fruit and rice loaves, Swiss rolls and products marking seasonal celebrations, such as hot cross buns and Christmas cakes.

As Mr Dickman aged and no one within the family wished to continue in the baking industry the business was sold, much to the sadness of pie lovers everywhere. Alas the street urchins cries of 'Dickman's pies are full of flies' no longer haunts Pitt Street and you can't help but wonder if the bakery had stayed open, would the saying 'Got to get to Greggs' be accompanied by 'Do dash down to Dickman's'…

(Thanks to Jayne Hamilton and George Thompson)

WOR SWEET SHOP – 1954
MICHAEL MCCARTHY

When sweets came off the ration back in 1954,
There were queues reet doon wor High Street te that welcome,
   open door.
Ah wuz seven an' quite skinny, ahll us kids were built the
   same,
There was just nee grub te build wuh up, wor parents weren't
   te blame.
Wor sugar allocation on the ration was quite bleak,
Wi' each person only gettin' just a horf a poond per week.
Yuh could get a poond o' jam as well, or two o' marmalade,
Or exchange that for a poond o' sugar, ahlwus strictly
   weighed.
So sweetness was a rarity, a treat te slowly savour,
Like gold dust in the kitchen, just te add some extra flavour.
Ah remember pinchin' sugar in a little paper wrap,
An' a stick o' Granda's rhubarb, as he sat an' had a nap.
But me Motha caught uz where ah hid, it didn't take hor lang,
An' tanned me backside as ah yelled, ah didn't horf get wrang.
But noo the sweet-shop's open, ah've thruppence here te
   spend,
Ah'm spoilt fer choice, as ah rejoice, the ration's at an end.
Ah stort off wi' some Trebor Chews, at fower fer just one
   penny,
There's Black-jacks an' Fruit Salad, ah divvent want that many.
A penny's worth o' acid drops is next upon me list,

Ah smile te think o' ahll those luv'ly flavours that ah've missed.
Horlicks tablets, sherbert dabs, an' chewy liquorice sticks,
Before wor local Woolworth's introduced thuh're Pick 'n Mix,
Just rows 'n rows o' big glass jars, wi' sweets o' every kind,
A wonderful assortment, ahll carefully aligned,
Wi' the labels on the front describin' ahll wor favourite treats,
A bairn's imagined paradise, a shop chock full o'sweets.
One penny left, so now ah choose a massive, red gobstopper,
It'll change it's colours as ah suck, my word that sweet's a
   whopper.
Ah can hordly get it in me gob, ah force it past me teeth,
Ah'm suckin' hard, ah want te see what colour lies beneath.
Ah take it oot, an noo ah see that stopper's tornin' blue,
It gans back in as ah begin te suck those colours through.
It's not quite 'everlastin'', as described upon the tin,
But it lasts a while, an' makes wuh smile, as it gans oot an' in.
Through blue te green, an' noo ah've seen that it's torned back
   te red,
Ah'm ahlmost done, ah've had some fun, there's nee mair te be
   said.
An' so ah'm plannin' te retorn, wi' next week's pocket money,
That sweetie shop, me favourite stop, me land o' milk an'
   honey…

SPECIALIST SHOPS

Sometimes you just need something a little less mainstream...

Henry Murton's shop on the corner of Grainger Street and the Bigg Market was an 'upmarket' department store selling expensive brands. I remember Aquascutam jackets, Slazenger tennis rackets and hockey sticks, proper Norwegian Bergan Rucksacks and skis. While Denton Cycles on Westgate Road did ski hire Murton's was perhaps the only shop in Newcastle to keep new skis with safety bindings - but they came at a price.

   Photography was a popular hobby in the 1950s and 1960s and Newcastle had several excellent retail outlets staffed by keen photographers who were always ready to help the beginner. Turners of Pink lane was 'famous' and I think documentaries may have been made about the company. The B &R Camera Exchange off the Bigg Market and Bonser's in the Bigg Market were also well known and helpful. Perhaps less well known was a shop selling Rank Kershaw Cameras situated opposite the War Memorial where the wall of Eldon Square is now. These cameras, which were made in Leeds, were of very high quality and not too expensive.

Ian Holloway

BELOW) TURNER'S ON BLACKETT STREET, 1972. RIGHT) 70S' ADVERT FOR TURNER'S.

HARRIS'S TRADING MENAGERIE

One of the most unusual shops in Newcastle before World War One was run by Charles Harris in Newcastle's Clayton Street for the sale of birds, beasts, reptiles and goldfish. Birds included budgerigars, parrots and canaries whilst among the beasts were hyenas, kangaroos and leopards.

Harris appears to have started in business at Shields Road in Newcastle's East End in the mid-1890s as a taxidermist, along with the selling of goldfish (at the rate of over 2,000 each week), canaries, budgerigars and parrots. At a later date he moved to larger premises in Clayton Street, where a four storey building and basement were converted into a menagerie containing a variety of exotic animals imported from distant parts of the world for clients that included 'local gentry' as well as 'foreign noblemen and royalty'.

Situated at 15 Clayton Street, the premises were close to its corner with Nelson Street that backed onto the Grainger Market and appear to have prospered until around 1913 when another proprietor is recorded as having taken over the business. After a few years

HARRIS'S TRADING MENAGERIE,
15, CLAYTON STREET.
BEARS, WOLVES, LEOPARDS, MONKEYS, HYENAS, PARROTS, and CANARIES.

Give us a Call.

The Tyneside Window Cleaning Company,
13 & 15, PERCY STREET, NEWCASTLE-ON-TYNE.

PAINT, WASHING, VARNISHING, and WHITE WASHING. Estimates Free. To ensure prompt attention, all orders must be addressed to W. J. PHILLIPS, PROPRIETOR.

the premises reverted back to other uses and at the time of writing the ground floor shop is occupied by a ladies dress retailer.

Very little is known about Charles Harris but it seems probable he may have been the source of the monkeys and colourful birds that for many years amused visitors at the Pavilion in Heaton Park, along with the brown bear that is reported to have entertained the public in a nearby circular pit.

Alan Morgan

TOP) HARRIS' ZOOLOGICAL GROTTO AT 15 CLAYTON STREET. RIGHT) THIS ADVERT APPEARED IN LOCAL PUBLICATIONS AS WELL AS IN NEWCASTLE UNITED'S MATCH PROGRAMME FOR NEW YEAR'S DAY 1901 WHEN WOOLWICH ARSENAL WERE THE VISITORS. MIDDLE) AN ADVERT FROM NORTHEN GOSSIP, SATURDAY 24 NOVEMBER 1900.

SHOPPING RITUALS AND RITES OF PASSAGE

We all have them and they're all unique; those family rituals which dictate your route around town when Christmas shopping or the first time you were allowed to go shopping with your friends on a Saturday afternoon: shopping can actually mean more than just a trip to the shops…

GOING TO THE CHAPEL … BUT TO THE SHOPS FIRST

I still remember my husband and I going to Jackson the Tailor to get measured up for our going away outfits when we got married in 1971. We stayed at the Royal Station Hotel overnight and picked up the bus the following morning to take us to the airport to catch our plane to Majorca. I still own the jacket but unfortunately I can't get into it nowadays.

Margaret Dinsdale

I chose my wedding dress at the last minute, the day before the wedding! It was July 1973 and I'd been to every shop I could think of, including the expensive Adam and Eve boutique on Ridley Place, but nothing was right. Eventually I found a navy blue ankle length floral dress which was just what I wanted, at Etam on Northumberland Street. It was £6.99. Much relief. I didn't think the wedding was that big a deal, but the right dress was important!

Annabel Flowers

Special occasions like weddings called for an outfit that hopefully no one else would turn up in. Where to go without paying a fortune? - Penny Plain opposite the Civic Centre. They sold lovely ethnic prints with mix and match items and as it was my sister-in-laws wedding and I was five months pregnant, I wanted something I felt comfortable in that wasn't from a maternity department. I found a lovely pinafore style dress and a loose fitting long sleeved top to go underneath. At my hairdressers, Venicia on Northumberland Street, hours before the wedding, they asked what my outfit was like and I explained it in great detail. They said they had the perfect new style that would complement my outfit and always up for something different I agreed to the new crimping style. It's fair to say the finished look was unique and no one else had the same style at the wedding. It was such a transformation that some Uncles were heard to whisper 'who is that woman with our nephew and where is Pat?' when they saw me on my husband's arm. Ahh! the choices fashion concious Newcastle offered to those willing to try them! The outfit did get a second wearing though: my husband wore the pinafore in a charity Boxing Day sea dip when they had to go in drag, and the blouse was put to use years later by my daughter as a cool hippy outfit for fancy dress.

Pat Rogerson

NEXT PAGE, CLOCKWISE FROM TOP LEFT. A 1951 ADVERT FOR C&A WINTER COATS. 2)SCALLON DISTINCTIVE TAILORING, 1938. 3) FENWICK'S WEDDING DRESS DEPARTMENT (WITH HEADS THIS TIME).

BRIGHT LIGHTS, BIG CITY...

Coming from Teesside, a shopping trip to Newcastle was always an exciting prospect. In the mid-80s the Haymarket area still retained some uncommercialised charm. Its Victorian shops and prefab cabins were a shabby contrast to the modern design of the new Eldon Square Shopping Centre. Next to the bus station was a row of shops. I would visit The Attic (later Attica of Old George Yard). It sold what is now called 'vintage', but in those days was anything old, generally pre-1970s, clothing and knickknacks. You always felt as if you would discover something special in the dim upstairs rooms. I still use a chenille door curtain I bought there in 1985. There was also a row of kiosk type huts that housed an early incarnation of Pet Sounds records and the Newcastle United supporters' shop, whose merchandise was limited to rosettes, badges, beer mugs and maybe one style of replica shirt. In the 80s, the match day crowds could be intimidating as hooliganism was common. It was always wise to return home before the final whistle.

Sarah Hall

Once a week my mother dressed up - putting on her best coat and hat instead of a headscarf, for her trip on the bus into town. In the school holidays, grumpily dressed in a dress, I went too. The main destination would be Bainbridge's on Market Street and the restaurant overlooking the Bigg Market, to meet friends, drink coffee and chat; I'd have an ice cream or an ice cream soda (preferably with cherryade).

To get to the restaurant you had to go through the children's shoe department... where we'd buy our school shoes, and one time some beautiful red open toed sandals. There'd then be the torment of the materials department and haberdashery downstairs; I'd have to wait for hours as my mother chose yards of cloth to make clothes, mostly mine, but she sometimes made fashionable evening dresses for friends and relations so there were bolts of silks, brocades and nets to examine. We might go over the road to Isaac Walton's, the school uniform suppliers, for dreary school things, but if you had your feet measured there for school shoes there was the X-Ray machine to stand on and see your foot revealed as a green skeletal image of a foot, which made up for the boredom.

Another boring chore was to wait in the queues at the market stalls in the Bigg Market for vegetables, though there was some entertainment from all the men shouting about their wares. There were lots of what seemed to me very large women with very large shopping bags and very bad tempers!

There was the School Furnishings at the bottom of Grainger Street where we bought the arithmetic revision books in the months before I took the eleven plus exam. I don't think I was very motivated, and was not keen to get them, but I remember the shop smelling of ink, darkness, and worry. We also bought an Osmeroid italic pen and Quink ink. I had a bad cold on the day of the exam, and didn't do too well!

Later, as a 60s' teenager, and finally allowed to go down town with friends and some ability to choose my own clothes, C&A Modes on Northumberland Street was my goal. Among those early purchases I remember I bought a grey and white striped t-shirt, some checked trousers and a shiny wide PVC belt. Before that Isaac Walton's came up trumps as I got my beloved black polo neck Beatles jumper there. But my mother made me lots of clothes: a blue denim skirt and shirt, and many mini-skirts. We had schoolgirl crazes for various items that became obligatory if you wanted to stay in fashion or even on the fringes of it in our school fifth form: very dark brown stockings, the shade was 'calvados', and blue nylon mackintoshes from C&A! Tights didn't appear until I was in the sixth form; by then boutiques were all over town, Handyside Arcade had been born and that's another story...

Annabel Flowers

It was 1964. In the sixth form in a small grammar school in West Yorkshire there was no advice about where to apply to university – yet we were allowed six choices. I might as well have stuck a pin in the list six times, and I have no idea to this day how I arrived at the shortlist, but at that point Newcastle University came in at number four. Some universities offered a conditional place without interview, whilst others required a formal visit, and this gave me the opportunity to go to cities I'd never been to before. My interview at Hull was a success, but I didn't much like the place. Kent University wasn't even built when I got there. The interview took place in a farmhouse soon to be demolished.

Newcastle was different. I loved the dramatic arrival by train, the bridges and the beautiful curved station. Crossing the road outside, I turned up Clayton Street but was rather disappointed by the shops and atmosphere. Where were the big name stores I expected in a big city? When I stopped to ask for directions, I had my first encounter with Geordie friendliness. 'Ee pet,' said the Andy Capp figure holding his cigarette inside his hand, away from my face, as he spoke. 'We love our students here. You should come. It's straight ahead next to the Haymarket.' My mood changed instantly from an uncertain naïve teenager to a much more confident would-be student. The interview didn't seem too threatening, and afterwards my interviewers took me to the top of the university's highest building for a view of the city. Then I noticed another main street of much more exciting shops and department stores. I could see along Northumberland Street with C&A's and Fenwick's, and began to think that Newcastle was the place to be.

Back to school and A levels. Newcastle offered me a conditional place which I accepted, so it moved to the number one slot, and my results confirmed that I was going to spend my days as a student on Tyneside.

It wasn't until my second year that I really got to know shopping in Newcastle. I shared a house in Fern Avenue,

LEFT) PICKING OUT A WEDDING DRESS IN FENWICK'S 1968.

Jesmond with four others and we had a rota for shopping and cooking. None of the convenience of the Jesmond supermarkets today's students have for microwaveable meals! William Low's store was no match for Tesco's, now in the same spot, but Barnett's Delicatessen on St George's Terrace sold the most delicious large white loaves with exotic poppy seeds on top. If students had to fill up on jam and bread, we did it in style! We lugged back bags of fruit and vegetables from the market because we were watching our grant money. At weekends we usually bought a large chicken as a change from the daily mince, and our friendly butcher always winked and threw on a couple of free sausages. I don't think the Grainger Market has changed much, apart from the sadly missed Robinson's second hand book stall where we often browsed after buying our food. This was of course the swinging 60s, so naturally we piled into the Club A Gogo on Percy Street at weekends. For some reason I remember the worn lino on the stairs, and then the exciting smoky gloom with groups like The Animals pounding out their beat. And what did we wear? If we were splashing out, the Elle Boutique virtually next door to the club, was the place of choice. I still have a dress I bought there in 1968, and I'll never part with it.

Not long ago I read a piece of research about students choosing to remain in the same city after graduation. Unsurprisingly, Newcastle (jointly with Bristol) came out on top. I am a part of this statistic. In fact, I'm still here!

Myra Robinson

When I arrived in Newcastle in 1994, Northumberland Street looked very different than it does now. Many shops have now disappeared - British Home Stores and C&A amongst them. Others such as Primark have arrived. The biggest difference has to be the pedestrianisation of the main road. It seems odd now to imagine the street busy with cars and buses and the many shoppers crowded onto the pavements on each side. Brenda and Margaret, my colleagues in the office determined that as a stranger to the city I should be properly initiated to Newcastle's shopping experience. The first decision to be made apparently was whether I was to be a Bainbridge's or a Fenwick's shopper - apparently I could not be both.

Bainbridge's was by far the easiest to navigate being the newer store built as part of the Eldon Square complex. Fenwick's however, with its rather grand Victorian frontage on Northumberland Street, wasn't. Escalators went up but there was no corresponding one down. There were two buildings joined, one on Northumberland Street which opened into Eldon Square, the other smaller building on Blackett Street next to what is now Waterstones. The two buildings met somewhere in the middle, but it took an expert to know how to navigate easily between the two buildings and the floors which were not exactly on the same level.

Brenda was defiantly loyal to Fenwick's and promised to instruct me in the mystery. And so it was that I was led through Fenwick's one afternoon and shown where all the hidden staircases were to be found, how to locate escalators up and separately the escalators down. It was many years later that refurbishment work was carried out to create the central banks of escalators which exist today. I have to say it feels as though some of the mystique has gone.

My initiation into Newcastle's shopping delights included a trip to the Grainger Market. What a delight of smells and colourful stalls. The Original Penny Bazaar was one of my favourites then. It still is today!

The Public Weigh House was also on the list of Newcastle

NEXT PAGE FROM TOP LEFT. 1) BHS ON NORTHUMBERLAND STREET,1990. 2) ETAM IN ELDON SQUARE, 1976. 3) JACKIE MILBURN (ON THE LEFT) REOPENING C&A FOLLOWING REFURBISHMENT, 1983.

experiences. I was instructed where to stand on the weigh scale in front of the counter. Discretion was all. The stony-faced man wrote down my weight on a tiny grey ticket which he passed across the counter, face down, his visage giving no clue as to whether my weight was high or low.

Our shopping trip began with lunch at Bimbi's on Pilgrim Street underneath the Odeon, now sadly demolished. The afternoon ended in the Tivoli restaurant at Fenwick's for afternoon tea. Twenty-three years on and I am still grateful to Brenda and Margaret for their introduction to Newcastle's shopping experience. Their love of the city and genuine delight at sharing it with a newcomer was just one of the many reasons I chose to stay in Newcastle and now count myself a proud adoptive Geordie.

Bea Charles

DEDICATED FOLLOWERS OF FASHION

Back in the Sixties I had a passion for fashion. I loved the mini skirt as well as hot pants. I couldn't wait for payday on a Friday knowing I could hit the town on Saturday and shop till I dropped at my favourite shop - C&A's. I still remember seeing a lovely jacket and trying it on, it fit like a glove and I fell in love with it. It never had a price tag on and as I was about to take it to the counter to ask how much it was a lady tapped me on the shoulder and said 'Excuse me but that's my jacket!' It still makes me laugh to this day.

Margaret Dinsdale

During the 80s, there was an outbreak of fluorescent coloured shoes and socks and accessories. I had a variety of bright footwear – orange, yellow and pink court shoes – which I used to buy in the really cheap shoe shops that lined Clayton Street, up towards Eldon Square. They also used to stock knock-off

'Frankie Says…' t-shirts, and those woven plastic 'basket' bags that were so popular. I bought an orange one of those on one excursion, which was utterly fabulous. I lined it with a plastic bag so I could take it to school so my stationery didn't fall out through the holes. And it matched my shoes, so I just had to use it.

Kirsty Ferry

WITH A LITTLE HELP FROM MY FRIENDS...

When I was a teenager in the 60s, I would meet friends at Mark Toney's in Grainger Street for an ice-cream, then we would go to Woolworths for sweets and make-up before ending up at Farnons looking for clothes. I loved going to Windows to buy the latest record, Bainbridge's for make-up and beauty products and C&A for clothes.

Linda Gallagher

I was a teenager in the 80s and, like most girls of my age, my friends and I used to haunt the likes of Top Shop, C&A, Dorothy Perkins and H&M. One of our favourite Saturday pastimes was to jump on the bus (the X51 or X52 would conveniently pick us all up on its route around Whickham) and we'd get off at the Cattle Market, more or less where The Centre for Life is now, and head into town. We would pick the most garish, ridiculous clothes simply for the joy of trying them on; sequinned boob tubes, ra-ra skirts, batwing tops – you name it. We would take armfuls of tat into the changing rooms and spend a happy half hour parading around in outlandish gear.

The changing rooms were horrifically communal. So the first thing you had to do was grab a corner that wasn't visible from the curtained off entrance, and then you'd basically huddle around a pile of clothes you knew you'd never ever buy - our

NEXT PAGE. TOP) 1980S' WINDOW DISLPAY OF MARCUS PRICE. RIGHT) C&A ON NORTHUMBERLAND STREET WITH ACCOMPANYING BAND, 1985.

mam's wouldn't like it and, let's face it, we probably didn't have enough cash anyway. Then you'd primp and preen, and compliment each other; swap the clothes around; compliment each other again – and then leave with an apologetic look at the long-suffering assistant outside: 'Sorry – not really what I was looking for.' And then head into the next shop and repeat it all again.

Kirsty Ferry

It was 1969 – the 'summer of love' and the line-up at Woodstock was something two fifteen-year-old schoolgirls could only dream about seeing. But listening to, well that was a different matter and J.G Windows in the Central Arcade was the place to start the Saturday shopping spree. How those patient shop assistants tolerated our every request from Ravi Shankar to Joe Cocker, Joan Baez to Santana. We must have whiled away a good two hours squashed into the acoustic booth, sharing the worn headphones and poking holes into the already pock marked and graffitied peg board. We usually bought a single each for a few shillings and if we had saved our pocket money – an LP.

The next stop was Handyside Arcade with its eclectic mix of shops with exotic names like 'Ultima Thule' where literary works by the Beat poets could be found – dangerously exciting to two impressionable teenagers. I remember buying Jack Kerouac's *On the Road* and a collection of Allen Ginsberg's poetry. Kard Bar was a must for badges and pop posters. I bought my first protest badge – a CND badge and a suggestive 'Save water - bath with a friend'. Our next stop would be 'Fynd' –a hippie heaven where nirvana could be achieved just smelling the incense and oils on sale which had permeated the velvet skirts, coats and jackets, unfortunately beyond our budgets. I did buy an old leather bag with tassels which, when it rained, smelt like camel dung – and a far cry from the designer brands worshipped by fifteen-year-old girls today.

Shopping in those arcades was exciting, tactile and educational. The shops were doorways into other cultures, far away places.

Sadly those shops have gone and now at the tap of a tablet or touch of a key we can shop, listen to music, but... there's something missing – the scent of patchouli.

Hélène C. Dolder

In my teens and early twenties going shopping in Newcastle was a social expedition with friends. We would spend hours in shops such as Tammy Girl and Internationale, browsing and buying as those shops fitted our teenage budgets. On some occasions we even queued outside HMV for hours on end to 'meet and greet' our favourite bands, something you don't see much anymore and teenage girls autograph books must be all the more sparse because of it! The shopping was complemented by getting something to eat and we somehow always managed to meet new people too! Completely different experience to my shopping experiences now with two young kids in tow!

Caroline McLaughlin

**TOP) LADY AT LORD JOHN, ELDON SQUARE, 1982.
RIGHT) ANGELA MERRITT WITH PHILLIP SCHOFIELD AT THE BBC SHOP.**

NORTH 'EASTER'NERS

The trip to C&A for our Easter clothes was more exciting than being exposed to x-rays from the foot measuring devices in the shoe shop. We got these at Easter as we always visited our relatives in Glasgow then, but it was always a North East custom to try and buy a new outfit for Easter. I got at least one new thing, it was either a good warm coat or a dress but owing to the pass down custom in families, it was not always both.

Elspeth Rutter

My grandmother had been a professional milliner in Durham and twice a year, in the 1950s, it was a huge treat to accompany her to Newcastle in search of a hat. The first visit was close to Easter Sunday and the second before Christmas. Our Easter visit was to buy outfits to wear on Easter Sunday at church. Suitably attired in our best clothes, wearing gloves - which no well-dressed woman would be without - my mother, aunt and I would meet her in Kirk Merrington, Co. Durham to travel by bus to Newcastle bus station located in what is now Times Square. The bus journey was part of the thrill: anticipating the shops, watching the changing scenery and chatting to the bus conductor and passengers.

On arrival our first port of call was the underground public conveniences at the bus station. I was relieved in more ways than one once that was over because we could at last head along Clayton Street to Farnons department store to inspect the hats and sometimes buy gloves.

We would look in every shop window en route to C&A in Northumberland Street. I remember one year buying a blue and white nylon dress and Easter bonnet and another year a bright yellow dress for Easter Sunday which was the day we would begin to wear summer clothes. The shops were well supplied with Easter hats and sandals- we believed it was unlucky not to wear something new on Easter Sunday.

1970S - KATY'S HAT SHOP, GRAINGER MARKET

Having tried on most of the hats, my grandmother would then suggest we visit Fenwick's.

I loved the huge counters and displays. Service in the shop was excellent, as was the selection of hats! We'd have lunch and my grandmother would offer my aunt and mother aspirin to stop the headache they were bound to get from walking around the shops. On the Christmas visit I would meet Santa - a terrifying experience even if he was the 'real' one- I was extremely shy and trying to speak to any unknown adult was a nightmare - but it had to be done! Window displays and Christmas decorations in Newcastle were the best in the region.

Suitably fed and medicated we'd continue to the dreaded Grainger Market to buy wool, ribbons and slides for my hair and buttons and trimmings for homemade clothes and to alter our hats. I still have an aversion to going in the market because it brings back the memory of how I loathed the sawdust, smell of blood and the dead carcasses hanging in the butchers' shops. My grandmother loved it and I think it was there she bought her alternative medicines. I would fervently hope we wouldn't stop there for something to eat, because I knew I'd be unable to swallow.

Binns or Bainbridge's was the next stop for the hat search and we might have tea, which was wonderful. The waitresses wore black dresses with frilled white aprons and caps and there was a silver tea service on a tray.

We would frequently return to the bus station without a hat for my grandmother. She would then decide which hat she should have bought. My poor aunt would then be sent back to buy the hat, once having to return to C&A in Northumberland Street - too great a trek for my grandmother and my little legs! We knew once we were home my grandmother would alter the hat to her own style.

In December the journey home involved counting Christmas trees and in the Spring anticipating wearing our new outfits on Easter Sunday. Needless to say my grandmother's large picture hat would look even better on Easter Sunday once it was adapted.

When I go to the village where my grandmother lived, older people still know me as the granddaughter of the lady who always wore incredible hats. I still love shopping in Newcastle, but avoid the Grainger Market!

Diane Phipps

FAME AT LAST

I still think of the time back in the 60s when TV cameras were in Newcastle filming young girls in miniskirts; I was looking in Marcus Price window and couldn't believe it when they asked if I would be one of them! All I had to do was walk over the crossing at Percy Street. I couldn't wait to watch it so rushed home, switched the TV on and settled down to watch my 'starring' role… but it was so quick that I blinked and missed it! Arghh!

Margaret Dinsdale

In 1949 my late husband, who was an optician, was working in a shop on the corner of Grey Street and Grainger Street, when a very pretty young girl came into the shop in great distress with a piece of grit in her eye. My husband promptly removed it and realised the young girl was Jean Simmons who was in Newcastle filming The Clouded Yellow with her co-star Trevor Howard. They had been shooting a scene in Grey Street with Jean Simmons driving an open top car when the grit blew into her eye and the filming had to stop.

Mrs A Herron

HUSTLE AND BUSTLE AT ISAAC WALTON'S, 1948.

IT'S A FAMILY AFFAIR

A trip to town was an event for our family when I was small. Day to day stuff could be bought locally, so excursions to the 'big' shops were always a bit of an occasion. There seemed to be a different shop for everything, and depending who I went with, the journey would always be an adventure. We had visits to 'specialist' shops for everything from pencils, paper and ink (T&G Allan's, where Jamie's Italian is now) school uniforms from Raymond Barne's (now Fitzgerald's in Grey Street) and bits for my dad's wireless from Aitken Bros in High Bridge (now a clothing shop).

My mum had an account at Binns, and another at Fenwick's, so she tried to avoid going to places like Bainbridge's and only under duress would she set foot in Marks and Spencer's (unless she was taking a short cut to the bus station), where, unlike Clarks shoe department in the more 'upmarket' emporiums, they actually sold shoes without measuring your foot first.

Once I escaped from my mum buying my clothes, the shop of choice was Lennard's on Clayton Street. They always seemed to have more stylish footwear...I liked visiting these places, with their vast shopping floors and seemingly endless corridors. And of course, as any child will tell you, going on an escalator is a thing of wonder. I'm told Newcastle's first escalator was in Boots on Northumberland Street (now a phone shop). I'm not certain if that's true, but I know we used to ride it over again, much to the annoyance of the store detective. The building itself is also fascinating if you take the trouble to look up at the facade – with its statues of John Marley, Thomas Bewick, Harry Hotspur and Roger Thornton.

Percy Street was another interesting street of shops. Apart from the Handyside Arcade, and its legendary Kard Bar, my attention was always taken by four completely different stores, standing side by side - Fagleman's the Jeweller; Henry Osborn's Tool Shop, Cockburn's Booksellers and Jeavon's musical instruments. An eclectic mix if ever there was, and sadly now replaced by the Eldon Garden shopping 'mall', but I visited all of them on a regular basis, and still have some of the purchases. My guitar, bought from Jeavon's in 1976 for the princely sum of £12 is a bit battered, but still rings out a tune, even if the player hasn't improved in forty years. Callers and Wenger's were also places of wonder, and Farnons was a great shop to get lost in. There was no chance of getting lost in Bus Stop or Plus Four, unless you got trapped behind a rack of jeans when a group of students came in to spend their grant cheques on cheesecloth and denim....

There are so many shops that are only distant memories in Newcastle - or anywhere else for that matter. Rumbelow's, Ratner's and Radio Rentals spring to mind. Binns and Bainbridge are no more; likewise Freeman Hardy & Willis and Etam, and more recently Littlewoods, BHS and Woolworths, Dolcis and Our Price. C&A still exists on the continent, and maybe someday will make a comeback. Until then I will have to pretend my favourite coat was bought on holiday....

Roland Finch

My mother-in-law always told my husband he was going in to the dungeons when she took him to Mark Toney's for a knickerbocker glory in the mid-1970s. She reckons promising him a trip there was the only way she could get him to go shopping with her.

Kirsty Ferry

NEXT PAGE, FROM TOP LEFT) 1) BABY ELEPHANT WALK, PROMOTING ROBINSON'S PET SHOP, ALONG CLAYTON STREET, 1968. 2) NEAR KATHERINE'S THE FLORIST, GRAINGER MARKET, 1970S. 3) WALKING THROUGH HANDYSIDE ARCADE, 1970S.

In 1951 shopping in Newcastle was an adventure. Mam, Dad and I took the No 17 United bus from the Coast to the Haymarket. Mam went shopping while Dad and I made a bee-line for Alfred and Warner's Toy Shop which was located where Blackwell's Bookshop is now. We gazed at the expensive Mamod steam engines and die-cast working model search lights. For a treat I might be invited to choose a Britain's 'lead' farm animal to add to my collection. Having met up with Mam we walked along Percy Street, perhaps looking at the toys in Boydell's Shop before having lunch at Carrick's restaurant. There were several in Newcastle and our choice might have been in Grainger Street. It was in a basement with small, square thick glass 'windows' set into the pavement. I remember the smoky atmosphere, the condensation on the ceiling and the heavy metal cutlery. The tea pot and hot water jug were thick metal, probably alloy, as steel was in short supply. I do not remember the main course but the soup was a distinctive brown (Windsor Soup?) and tasted and smelled meaty but may not have had much meat in it. For pudding there was a choice of sponge and custard or vanilla ice cream served in a distinctive heavy metal ice cream cup with a wafer biscuit.

What exciting days these were! Other bookshops I remember were Waughsin on Ridley Place, near the City Hall, and The Students' Bookshop first of all at the corner of Claremont Road then later in the premises of Alfred and Warner's. The Students' Book shop was an 'academic bookshop' with text books from wall to wall and from floor to ceiling. By 1958 The Model Shop Newcastle was a Saturday shopping 'must' especially after they opened the new shop in Blenheim Street deliberately styled in the form of an aerodrome control tower.

Ian Holloway

Newcastle's C&A was the source of our Winter coats. When we were younger, my aunt who was a dressmaker had made

them. We hated her last effort, green with velvet collars, and hats that buttoned under the chin with a cheerful band around the face which was supposed to make you look like flower petals. The flower band was constantly falling over onto our faces and even mother saw that this wouldn't do after a man sitting opposite to us in a tram could barely stifle his laughter. My father gave my mother extra money for coats and off we sallied in pursuit of our goal. Even when very young we wanted to choose them ourselves.

In a generation in which my grandmother (and Queen Victoria), said that children should be seen and not heard, my mother made the final choice. Quality and practicality were of course her goals. I wanted bright blue with a velvet collar, no way! It was to be a plain blue woollen coat with a matching hat. Two pieces for the price of one. Off to church and she used to pull it over my head very tightly to stop it slipping and that left a red wheal on my forehead when it was removed. I found a way of getting rid of it: as Catholics we went to our parish church, St Mary's Cathedral on Sundays. For a child of five or six the service was long and at some point I felt faint and pulled my hat off; mother blamed my near fainting on the hat and I never wore it again… I had exaggerated the fainting feeling! When older we still bought coats at C&A right into our college days, also blouses and skirts. Fenwick's was a competitor for our money, although often dearer, they had more fashionable things. Mother never shopped at Fenwick's: too expensive! C&A also had a large hat department upstairs.

Once I went with my mother to C&A to buy a hat for a wedding when I was a teenager. It was hilarious trying them on, the more unsuitable the better. We laughed so hard we were almost asked to leave, seeing the assistant scowl we went voluntarily.

Many years later with my daughter we took my mother, then in her eighties, to the Metro Centre. Sitting in her wheelchair she tried on hats. She was full of joy and for her I think the years flew

199 GUINEAS (ABOUT £2800 IN TODAY'S PRICES) FOR PERSINA LAMB AT MARCUS THE FURRIER, 1950S.

back and she was young again, back to the twenties when she and her friends made their own from felt shapes and cut and decorated them to the latest fashion. It is one of my happiest memories and it briefly relieved the tedium of the residential home where she spent her last eighteen months. There were also numerous small hat shops in town, although I'm sure they didn't make the exorbitant profits that modern hatters make.

Patricia Bensdorp-Clark

Around 1962 I pestered my parents for a pair of 'Louie'-heeled shoes; the first pair of heels I'd have bought for me as I would have been around fourteen. Saturday morning came and off we went to town; starting at the bottom of Northumberland Street we worked our way through every shoe shop asking for these shoes with no luck. Bearing in mind this included shops like Barratt's, Dolcis and Saxone as well as the big department stores Fenwick's, C&A (Dad left us at this point having lost the will to live) Littlewood's and British Home Stores. We then moved onto Grainger Street; more shoe shops, Bainbridge's and Binns, then all the way down to Wenger's. Time was running out: it was my cousin's birthday and we were invited to tea at my aunts in Byker so had to give up in order to get there for five o'clock. Defeat! My aunt couldn't believe my parents would do this; as she put it 'I'd have slapped her legs and made her choose something else!' Fortunately my mum understood, as like myself she always looked for something different and after a few weeks we found said shoes in a lovely cream colour in Timpson's on Grainger Street.

Pat Rogerson

When I was a little girl, my aunts lived with us. Nowadays they would have lived in a flat together, but the girls stayed with their parents until they married. Lacking parents, they became part of the older sister's family. My aunties were pretty, happy girls in their twenties, Doris slender and as straight as a tulip, looking a bit like Susan Sarandon. Lily was more exotic with the dark eyes and hair of a smouldering senorita.

Their interest in clothes, hairstyles and make-up was passed on to me almost by osmosis. They influenced me greatly as I absorbed their behaviour as naturally as breathing.

The girls went dancing regularly, wearing wonderful gowns and high heeled shoes that Ginger Rogers would have been very envious of. The dresses, rustling taffetas, slinky crepe or shimmering satin, soft as snowflakes, were breath-taking. Everything was always prepared the day before each event. The luscious gowns hanging on our workday cupboard doors made the humble room look more mundane than ever. I was forbidden to go near and had enough respect for the fairytale clothes, and my glamorous aunts, to gaze awe-struck as those who ate the loaves and fishes. I rarely saw these lavish gowns more than twice, but knew they came from 'Jacky Fish', a family friend who owned a shop. His surname was Heron but my aunties only knew of 'baked herring', hence the translation 'Jacky Fish'. I was much older before realising this was a second hand shop, though dealing in high class merchandise. My aunties were not just good friends but good business for the owner.

Sometimes as a special treat, I joined the forays for potential replacements. The shop on Percy Street had two large windows which curved round to the centrally placed door. Inside to the left, the shop was devoted to gents wear and military uniforms. The right side was an Aladdin's Cave for the ladies. A wall of men's suits and overcoats, hanging from tightly packed rails, formed a fairly solid backdrop to the main shop. It was possible to slip through this barrier, with its stifling smell of musty tweed, to enter a more homely area. Here was a huge kitchen where a friendly fire burned brightly, the kettle always ready for a fresh pot of tea. Kitty, the bustling lady assistant, displayed the beautiful dresses especially for my aunties.

After tea came the trying on. Lily and Doris preened and twirled on the clippie mat before making their final choice. My earliest years were spent in this exotic whirl, where nail varnish, flowers, false hair and jewellery were as vital as the outfits. The auntie's discarded high heels were my passion. I clopped about happily in shoes that had graced the many fine ball rooms Newcastle then had to offer. Cinderella's glass slippers couldn't have pleased me more.

Jane Smailes

When I was much younger, one of my favourite shops design-wise, was Mawson, Swan and Morgan, opposite Grey's Monument. I don't actually remember what it sold, but I have a feeling it was stationery, and I've always been a fiend for stationery. I just loved the staircase inside the building – I used to pretend it was a grand house and I was sweeping down the stairs in a long dress! There was also an old bookshop my Dad used to take me in, and we'd spend hours poking around the shelves, looking at the second-hand books. I think it was on Westgate Road, up from the ABC Cinema. It was quite dark and dim inside – but very safe and very lovely and we had some wonderful afternoons hidden away in there.

Kirsty Ferry

AN OUTFIT FIT FOR A QUEEN

On the 1st December 1990 I needed an outfit for the launch of British Antarctic Survey Ship the *James Clarke Ross*. However, the outfit didn't perform quite the way I expected...

The Commander, who people called KK, jumped out of his chair and straightened his tie. 'No, you go.' He looked at his watch. 'You'll have two hours before the shops close.'

He walked towards the kettle, combing the loose strands of his curly grey hair back. After working endless hours for launch day, he was ready for a well-earned break. It was now so close to the day the Queen would arrive at Swan Hunter's shipyard.

I pulled on my coat and hat and moved out of the office, before the phone rang and delayed my exit. As I stepped out of the building I could hear the tapping of metal and wires chiming in the wind, the familiar smell of molten metal drifted around every corner. And I could see the *James Clarke Ross* standing tall in the slip way, dwarfed by the larger warships. I turned and headed up the bank.

The Metro stopped a little further up and it would take me into the centre of town. I didn't know what I was looking for and I couldn't decide where to start. At that time, clothes were still quite conservative, to digress was a courageous move. Many little boutique shops had appeared around this time, selling more expensive and exclusive labels than the high street stores. The shops were all positioned around the back streets of

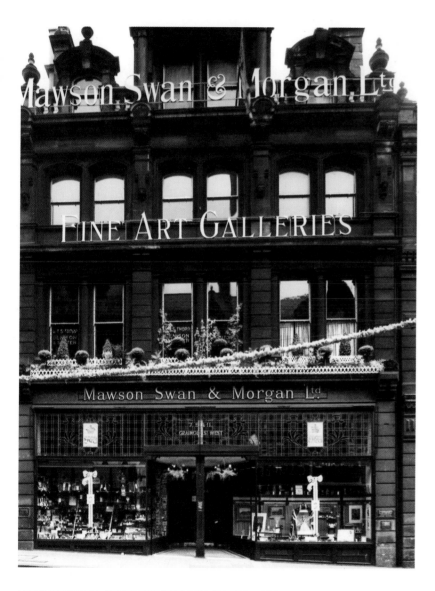

A Happy Xmas "Eve"

The delighted Recipient of a

Mawson Hand Bag

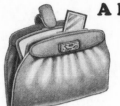

Beautiful Navy Calf Bag of uncommon design . . . . lined grey corded silk : Roomy divisions and strap at back. Quaint tab fastening with Prystal Ornament . . . . . Price **47/6**

Blue Crushed Calf Bag, highly polished, 12″ long at base, exceptionally wide opening. Fitted with inner division, mirror and thumb loop. Smart lining of striped silk **78/6**

Distinctive looking Green or Red **Morocco Pochette** with zip fastening and thumb loop of Real Crocodile. Dainty silk lining and fitted mirror, purse, etc., or in Grey with lizard loop. Price **23/6**

The Materials . . Colourings . . . Adroit Fashioning . . . and Fastenings are largely responsible for the Reputation of our . . .

HAND BAGS for

Smartness and Style.

Morocco Pochette with zip fastening and button and buttonhole decoration, lined silk and fitted purse and mirror. Price **32/6**

Fashionable **Tapestry Pochette**; pretty colour blendings, with inner division and mirror. Lined silk, thumb loop and smart bar clasp. Wonderful value at **7/6**

Our famous Silk Bag in dainty colours **5/9** ☞

A Handsome Bag of Velvety Black Douva Calf with real Python thumb loop and frame. Decorative carved knob fastening. Lined silk and fitted with divided inner division and combined mirror and powder case. One of our most exquisite patterns. Price **59/6**

LEFT) MAWSON, SWAN AND MORGAN ON GREY STREET, CURRENTLY A POSH BURGAR CHAIN.
RIGHT) LOVELY HANDBAGS FROM MAWSONS - 1950S.

the city, which added to their charm, somehow exclusive to those in the know. Their window displays straight from trend setting magazines offered a slice of 'conservative' but 'hip' fashion.

I can't remember what took me down Dean Street, where a few shops existed on the developing Quayside, feet away from the base of the Tyne Bridge. But, I found myself in the fancy shop on the corner called Tiger Tiger, sliding velvet coat hangers along the sparse rails. It was a tiny shop and a girl sat behind the counter with a television screen high on the wall, not paying any attention to the soundless images. She looked at me and smiled.

'You looking for anything in particular?' She put down her pen and came across.

Once I told her why I needed an outfit she became very animated, and picked out dresses, skirts, trousers and tops. A big heavy curtain was pulled back where she hung all the items on pegs and directed me inside.

I tried on all the clothes, I didn't feel comfortable in any. I pulled on a pair of trousers which were high waisted with a tight buttoned bodice which I thought were quirky and different from the typical Princess Diana look. We were in the 90s now and with women's lib, emancipation and equal rights I didn't have a problem wearing trousers for lunch with the Queen. Though I suspect others could disapprove. But, I loved them, they looked like something a Spanish matador would wear. I had a beautiful Paul Smith, purple velvet bolero jacket which I had bought from Jules. All I needed was a Spanish hat. I would give the castanets a miss, and this would be a truly dramatic outfit.

The day of the launch arrived, everywhere had an intoxicating smell of fresh paint and all the toilets smelled of peach air-freshener. A toilet, close to reception, was refurbished for Her Majesty's personal use with fresh flowers placed inside. And flowers adorned the reception area.

Everyone had dressed with care and we shone with smiles of nervous excitement. There's always something at these events which needs to be done, but we had exhausted every eventuality and we needed to get into action.

The Commander told me that morning, that I was to be in one of the limousines in the Queen's cavalcade. I was so ignorant of any necessary etiquette, it didn't faze me. Obediently I climbed in. The chauffeur stared forward, unaware I was a small nobody, travelling behind the Queen's car. I wanted to shout at the top of my voice, 'Look at me!' And, how I wish, I could have had the entire experience on video. As we travelled through the streets of Newcastle with police motorbikes escorting us, we passed through a sea of red, white and blue flags, the crowds waved, and traffic drew to a halt, as we sailed through.

Minutes later, I learned why ladies of high stations are taught how to climb in and out of limos. Because, once the car stopped, my door was opened, I had to get out. The exit was so low, if I had been wearing a dress, modesty would have forced me to bring both my legs around. But I was wearing trousers and I stretched my leg onto the yard, pushed my bottom low to catapult myself out.

I could see nothing as panic blinded me... and I felt the seam in my trousers rip. I put my hand over my bottom, I could feel the silk of my underwear through the stray threads from the

NEXT PAGE, FROM TOP LEFT. 1) 70S' FASION ON NORTHUMBERLAND STREET. 2) PULLING THE TROLLEY DOWN NORTHUMBERLAND STREET, 1974. 3) EXCLUSIVE ELEGANCE FROM BOOKS FASHIONS, 1950S. 4) AN ADVERT FROM NORTH EAST TIMES, 1983. 5) LOOKING FAB OUTSIDE THE BEEHIVE IN THE BIGG MARKET, 1970S.

Fashion and Shopping of the Times

Photographed in our own Showroom

now open seam of the coarser material. I stopped breathing, I felt the heat rising in my face and the cheers of the crowd. All eyes were on the Queen, nobody would notice.

I was there to make sure the day went smoothly, I couldn't concern myself with irrelevant details, and I had no option, but to continue with my duties. We went into the auditorium and the place was awash with dignitaries and MPs and Security. I chatted and checked everyone had drinks and canapés, I moved around the room, my bottom clenched tight to disguise the rip in my trousers, checking there was nothing which needed attention. I was handling this well. All was going like clockwork. Then I felt a tap on my shoulder.

'All right?' It was the Commander, kind and thoughtful. 'I've organised for you to be presented to the Queen, alongside some of the staff from the British Antarctic Survey'.

It was unexpected and he would have sweet talked someone into allowing me this honour. He raised his eyebrows and nodded his head.

'Oh...' was my response... The Commander would have noticed the flash of fear in my eyes, he would have thought I was nervous... and I was, for all the wrong reasons. But, here was the man who instilled in me, the belief, everything was possible... and my shoulders were broad. 'We are like rubber ducks' he would say, 'push us down and we bounce back'.

I knew I had to address the Queen as mam as in ham not Maam as in palm, I had to keep everything brief, smile and curtsy.

I dutifully stood up with the rest of them, wondering how I could curtsy without my undergarments being exposed. But there was no escaping the fact, my knickers would be presented to all the MPs and dignitaries standing behind me. I watched her coming along the line, she was wearing the bespoke broach which we had crafted for her, it was based on a broach I wore by Rennie MacIntosh. She was getting nearer

and nearer, I could hear the people behind me laughing and chatting. What was a girl to do?

The Queen was more important than any one standing behind me, and if they were gentlemen, they would avert their eyes. The Queen was tiny, and she asked me in her Queen voice if I had organised the day and I explained that I had worked alongside the Commander. And of course I curtsied.

The excitement of meeting the Queen, would have been exhilarating, but we had to now get the guests to the Civic Centre where we would have lunch and watch the Royal Guards 'Beating the Retreat'. Once there and the guests were sorted I asked our company chauffeur, Joe, if he could do me a favour, and drive me into town.

'It's a shop called Tiger Tiger not very faraway, Joe.' I felt a fraud it wasn't company business and so I explained, I needed another pair of trousers.

'Of course pet' he laughed.

I jumped in the black company Mercedes and we chatted on the way to the quayside. Once there, Joe parked outside the shop and I jumped out.

The girls stood staring at me as I opened the door. One of them pointed up to the television, 'We were just watching... the launch on television.' They hesitated unable to understand why I was there.

I explained my predicament and just as quick they explained they didn't have another pair.

I was crest fallen. One girl reached into the drawer. 'There's a needle and thread, you could use'.

I grabbed hold of it and headed into the changing room where I stitched up the hole. As I sat in the changing room, aware this could only happen to me they chatted and I relayed my meeting with the Queen. Once sewn up, I thanked them and ran back to the car.

'Thank you Joe! For rescuing me'.

He smiled at me. 'We'll say we were dealing with the press'. 'Sounds a good one'.

He winked and we headed back to the Civic Centre, just as everyone was following the Queen, to be seated for lunch.

I still have my trousers, but Tiger Tiger is no longer there. It, like so many of the small boutique shops, has morphed; some sell different merchandise or have become coffee shops and restaurants. But Tiger Tiger will forever burn bright in my memory.

Sonja Hughes

NEW YEAR, NEW ... HOT WATER BOTTLE

I used to make my annual pilgrimage to Boots the Chemist (as it was known and long before it became the 'department' store it is now) a few days after New Year's Day. The reason being is that a friend of my mother would always buy my sister and I a £1 Boots gift voucher for Christmas. Trying to find anything of interest would take a good hour of rummaging around leaving no stone unturned. The inevitable result was an impatient mother and two children who unanimously decided, once again, to go for a hot water bottle each. It was either that or a toothbrush, a bottle of Lucozade or a couple of those 'medical' lollies that allegedly provided vitamin C.

There was not the vast selection of hot water bottles that one sees nowadays. There was a choice of colours, one or two different textures and whether to have one with a safety top or without. The ones that came with a cover (and therefore didn't burn you as quick) were out of our price range.

Simon Carey

TOP) SONJA HUGHES MEETING THE QUEEN AND A RATHER PARANOID LOOKING SECURITY GUARD. RIGHT) BOOTS ON NORTHUMBERLAND STREET, 1975.

SPINNING DISCS

As a music-obsessed teenager at school in the 1970s my record shopping was limited to a few shops in Scunthorpe – Boots, W H Smith, good old Woolworths and the independent Record Village. When I became a student at Newcastle University my vinyl horizons expanded. Obviously there were the usual suspects – W H Smith and Boots but, joy of joys, there was a Virgin Megastore in Eldon Square. What a fantastic place to invest my student grant in the wonders of late 70s and early 80s music (Bowie, Human League, Heaven 17, not to mention the odd meander into prog rock!). There were also a number of independents and second hand record shops (and of course charity shops) and these were duly investigated and they too would relieve me of cash (no credit cards for me in those days!). As my taste became a bit more esoteric, I started seeking out 12" disco singles and albums, particularly if they were hot imports from the United States. Surprisingly it was Callers, a furniture shop on Northumberland Street, which had a record department that was a wonderland of imported vinyl. My collection certainly got bigger and better there – Sylvester, Phyllis Nelson, Tantra – were a few of the names to conjure with. Windows in the Central Arcade, as well selling top end Bang & Olufsen hifi, was also a good place to indulge a love of vinyl.

By the time I left the university in 1981 my record collection was extensive. Sadly over the years, new technology – dvds, iTunes, etc. - has whittled down my collection to a shadow of its former self. The untold rarities that were shifted off to second hand shops can only be mourned and never replaced!

Brendan Thorpe

By the late 1970s Eldon Square had taken its hold on Newcastle city centre and would have you know it was the shopping destination that offered everything… but outside its huge air-blasting doorways, there was plenty of prime space in good use. It took me a while, but I gradually discovered a whole other world away from chain stores and branding that formed, what I came to recognise as, some kind of Saturday circuit of record shops that I would tread each week throughout my early teens.

Early 1979, I was 13. So far I had dabbled with buying a few singles, but now it was time to get serious… I wanted to buy albums! *Plastic Letters* by Blondie and *Armed Forces* by Elvis Costello & The Attractions. I looked in all the shops to find the cheapest copies… Callers for Blondie and Windows for Costello. I would love these records and play them repeatedly and soon started shopping around to buy the bands' earlier releases.

I quickly realised that WH Smiths, Boots, John Menzies and Woolworths - who all had sizeable record sections at the time - only stocked the charts. It was much harder to get a single in the picture sleeve from these shops - the sleeve was such an important part of owning a record. I didn't want a single by Blondie or even the Boomtown Rats in a plain sleeve. You had to be careful in Woolworth's. Even if they did have the picture sleeve they had a bizarre way of displaying singles… it must have been somebody's job to punch a hole in the top left corner of each sleeve. They displayed their singles like they displayed their sweets… dangling on spikes! Callers, who had a serious record department, were far from faultless. If you bought their last copy of a single the picture sleeve would be folded down one edge so it could be squeezed into a seven inch cardboard sleeve and shelved behind the counter. This probably helped with their stock reordering system, but not so good for the buyer.

As I approached 14, after repeated late nights listening to John Peel, I developed a taste in music that couldn't be satisfied by shops that did records as a side-line. It had to be a specialist shop. Despite being in Eldon Square, on High Friars,

Virgin Records was an early favourite. It was really dark inside and had a spiral staircase going to a gallery section… but it was really dark! The walls were painted black and the only lighting seemed to be thin beams shining on the record displays. It was stunning… probably a shoplifters' delight… and certainly the antithesis of the fluorescent lighting in other shops. Virgin had wire display bins heaped upwards with new releases. In March 1979, that's where I found (and paid for!) a new twelve single by Graham Parker. Later that year, the store expanded and changed beyond recognition - it became much brighter and was all on one level. They still had amazing displays though. When Public Image released Metal Box - in a flat round tin - they had so many copies spread out that it reminded me of the cake stands in the kitchen section at Fenwick's. In September 1979 Virgin took out a full page advert in Sounds announcing limited copies of the new Slits LP *Cut* sold around the country in their shops would be signed by the band. I made sure I was one of the first in the shop that Saturday! Chasing down the sudden explosion of limited edition records in 1979 became quite a challenge. I would seek out records like the Members Sound of the Suburbs in clear vinyl; the Skids Into The Valley on white vinyl and even an orange triangular shaped disc by John Cooper Clarke. (Thankfully, it had a record player friendly circular section in the middle that was exactly seven inches.) Fittingly, the record was called *Gimmix*. By the time records were released commenting on the trend; its time was almost up.

By then my Saturday routine was set. Get on the bus at Whickham by 9.30am. Arrive at Marlborough Crescent and then a hurried walk to Virgin for 10am. I might stop off at HMV at the bottom of Northumberland Street. Not so good there though. Probably better to go a few hundred yards up Northumberland Street and straight into Callers. Although it was a department store selling furniture and holidays they had a large and well run record department. They were fantastic for limited editions… the freshest of which would be in small, quickly dwindling, piles on the floor behind the staff. The staff seemed quite disdainful of the music I liked - as if it was trifling.

Later, I learnt they were great authorities on American soul music and they stocked an excellent range of 60s music that I had yet to discover… but that was for later. Right now, it was full pelt to Listen Ear on Ridley Place (The location taken by Volume Records in the 80s.) This shop was small and very different to the others because it didn't stock the top 40 singles as a matter of course - only the ones they liked. Listen Ear specialised in the punk and post-punk records that had me so taken from hearing them on John Peel's show. This was the place to buy the Glaxo Babies, Neon Hearts and The Mekons. They stocked gig tickets and fanzines too… which turned out to be independent music magazines, often

locally produced. They were largely amateurish looking things photocopied onto A4 sheets, but all the more interesting for that and had interviews with bands less likely to be written about by national publications. Listen Ear was run and owned by people who were really into this music. It had a much more relaxed feel than the other shops and they didn't seem to mind if you hung around, leaning on their racks, waiting to see who came in for a chat. Later in the day, as the crowds appeared, you'd shuffle around in what standing space there was. I took a breather here and chatted to familiar faces from previous weeks. 'Siouxsie Fan' was somebody I saw most weeks. She was always friendly and after a while I got to know she was called Stella... That's when I started to recognise there was a circuit that many of us were treading each Saturday... It was during these conversations that you heard about new releases coming up or something you might have missed in a previous shop... then you'd dash back! It wasn't a complete love-in though... I was in Listen Ear in late '79 and met up with Toot, my punk schoolmate. There was a white label LP playing. Kevin, behind the counter, asked Toot a little pointedly, "Do you like this?" "Nah," Toot replied. There was a pause then Toot resumed, "When's the new Clash album coming out?" I cringed. The music was new to me too, but I recognised Joe Strummer's voice. The LP turned out to be an advance copy of the Clash's London Calling. Toot walked right into that one.

Each Saturday, later in the day when my money was low or all gone, I'd already be planning what to buy the next week. J G Windows was always a good place for that... they were the only shop with listening booths. There were two of them... in the basement on the left as you walked in. Each was big enough for one person. I asked to listen to the Cure's first album and then stepped under the small fibreglass enclosure shaped like a bubble. It wouldn't have looked out of place at the airport with a phone under it... except these were very scruffy; the plastic might have once been transparent, but was now quite yellow.

The walls were white plywood with small shallow holes to trap the sound - two speakers mounted in the walls. But that enclosure must have had special powers of persuasion because everything I listened to I eventually bought.

Records were my main interest, but occasionally I was tempted by the badges and posters in the Kard Bar, located in the Handyside Arcade. The arcade itself was surreal. It seemed to have moods - its glass roof made it as dark or as bright as the day outside. There were street lights in the middle of the footpath. I'm not sure I ever saw them lit. How did this place get here? (I know now it was a beautiful Edwardian structure. Over time, it adapted and, full of independent shops, it thrived during the 60s and was still doing good trade in the 70s and 80s. In 1987 it was swallowed whole and regurgitated as a completely bland adjoin to Eldon Square). I recall a wonderful place where tribes of punks, mods, hippies and heavy metal kids mingled freely. Aside from the main Kard Bar shop, for a while, they also had a record shop opposite that was rarely open, probably only on a Saturday afternoon... and then only if you nagged them to open it. While I was waiting, I'd press my face against the glass looking into the small drawers displaying a fantastic selection of independent singles. Being able to see them lying flat - to see their sleeves - not just a mass of meaningless spines on a shelf made them all the more tempting.

Some Saturdays, and you had to get your information on the grapevine to know about this; the routine would be turned on its head because there was a band you wanted to see coming to the City Hall. The place to start that day was in the box office queue on Northumberland Road. How far beyond the swimming baths would the queue reach before we were allowed in? If I went to get a ticket for Penetration and the street was full of heavy metal kids then I'd probably arrived on the wrong day!

Many Saturdays, I'd have already been all the way round

town once but found it too exciting to leave behind for a whole week so I'd revisit shops from earlier. Back to Virgin. Dig a little deeper in their racks. By 3pm it was bursting with leather jacket punk boys. All chat. Standing away from the counters. If I still had any money left I'd join the seemingly endless queue to buy singles.

My sense of there being a Saturday circuit of record shops that a number of us were treading each week was confirmed a few years later when I met people in clubs who had also been keen record buyers and more recently, it's been a topic discussed online. What we had in Newcastle probably wasn't unique and likely typical of most major cities around the UK. Probably also typical… when I left school, my visits were more sporadic and the weekly ritual was broken. Aged 13 to 16, I had a good run. They were crucial years, after which I felt and looked 'very changed' and I think very affected by my experiences. It had somehow been much more than shopping for pieces of plastic. At the time it had seemed to be everything in the world that mattered and perhaps for a while it was.

Simon Mckay

Newcastle had the largest and best stores in the region, which provided a Mecca for the more discerning shoppers who poured into town at weekends. I used to go to the town on a Saturday just to mingle with the shoppers and be part of the excitement. I bought my gramophone records at Windows or Alderson and Brentnall, or at one of the many other record shops such as The Wireless Shop or Jeavons on Pudding Chare. Records then were still heavy, breakable and spun round at 78 revolutions per minute but the long player was being introduced. It played lightweight flexible records on a turntable that spun at only 33 rpm. I well remember with what fascination a crowd of us stood outside Windows Record Store in the Arcade watching a turntable revolving at 33 rpm in the window. No sound, just the turntable going round and round at a speed at which with a little training you could read the label on the record that was playing!

Joe Pegg

SIGNS OF THE TIMES

The 1970s was a graphic designer's dream time with the trend for re-designing logos and images throughout the retail sector. The buzz phrase at the time was 'corporate identity', which meant designing a logo or brand image and applying it throughout a company's shopfront, stationery, signage, advertisements, price tickets, vehicles, uniforms and any other publicly seen items relating to the business.

Newcastle saw an ever changing face to its shops during the 1960s and 1970s with the locally owned boutique clothes shops that sprang up all along High Bridge and Bigg Market. This part of the city became the trendy shopping area of Newcastle, with such names as 'Boy meets Girl', Geordie Cobbler, Cream, Bezique, Plus Four and further up Grainger Street, Marcus Price and Bus Stop.

Newcastle soon had its own version of the Kings Road and Kensington Market in London. 1960s' Newcastle teenagers and students had previously had to travel in order to find 'trendy gear'.

With the opening of Eldon Square, the focus of clothes shopping gradually moved to Old Eldon Square, Ridley Place and the top of Northumberland Street, with shops such as Victoria & Albert, Great American Panthouse and Wildes Hairdressing. A few of the larger local based boutiques such as 'Boy meets Girl' and Plus Four, were able to open 'flagship' stores within Eldon Square. Many of these businesses had commissioned Badge Group Design to re-design their shopfronts, logos and corporate images during this period, such as 'Boy meets Girl', Bezique and Greggs.

Christopher Baglee

IN A TIGHT SPOT

Stockings were an expensive item in the 1950s. Silk stockings were the most expensive and lisle stockings were cheaper at about four shillings a pair. Most of us wore lisle.

Nylon stockings were just coming onto the market. If you knew an American or Canadian serviceman you might be lucky and get a pair. By 1950, however, most of the servicemen had been posted home. You could send away to Gibraltar where stockings were available for 15 shillings a pair, plus excise duty.

As a junior typist my wage was 35 shillings a week. Fifteen shillings of this was my pocket money. Bus fares to work, trips to the pictures, clothes, possibly a magazine as a treat – 15 shillings didn't go very far. No nylon stockings for me!

There was, however, an alternative to stockings. Leg make up from the chemist was cheap. I saved even more money by making my own from calamine lotion and a few drops of Mam's gravy browning. My parents didn't approve so I had to slip out without them noticing my 'sun tanned' legs. It was chilly in winter and it washed off in the bath so it was never a perfect solution.

Mabs Taylor

You used to wash your nylons every night and roll them in a towel to help them dry. If you got a ladder you could go to Fenwick's to get them repaired. There was a little girl who sat at a machine that picked up the stitch and reworked it. It cost about 6d a ladder.

Norah Coombes

You'd carry nail polish to stop ladders in your nylons. It would stick to your leg, but it didn't matter if it pulled the hairs on your leg when you took them off! As long as the ladder didn't go any further – nylons were expensive.

Mary McArdle

BEAR BRAND TIGHTS AND STOCKINGS IN FENWICK'S 1957.

THE WORKERS SPEAK OUT: JOBS IN SHOPS

For many of us our first foray into the working world was via a Saturday job in a shop; which could either spark a love of retailing to last a lifetime or put you off for life…

My first shop job was when I was fifteen, I was at Art College and my friend and I went for Christmas jobs at Woolworths on Shields Road. She got the job there and I got a job at the Northumberland Street branch. I can't remember cleaning floors but I had to clean the counters every day. The big sales floors had shelving on the outside walls and the rest of the sales areas were islands of flat counters. If anything was shoplifted or if our till didn't balance at the end of the day, we were expected to make up the loss! Our coats and bags were locked up during the days and pockets were frowned upon. We wore overalls which I presume had no pockets. Even though staff were not trusted, we had to be very formal and call each other by Miss, Mrs or Mr. There would be at least one supervisor on each floor who floor walked. This was as much to check on our behaviour and the neatness of our counters as it was to stop shoplifters. We were not allowed to chat to our fellow workers and could only talk to each other in the staff room at lunchtimes.

At all times we were to look busy at our counters and of course be ready to help customers. However it was a holiday job and it meant money of my own. We were all brought up to have a healthy respect for money and did jobs at home for our pocket money; cleaning shoes, ironing, cleaning the windows and mirrors and vacuuming. The worst job was cleaning out and resetting the coal fire. It took ages to get our hands clean afterwards.

Elspeth Rutter

As a young teen I worked as a Saturday girl in Woolworths Cafe on Northumberland Street in the early 1970s. I loved it. The money was good. I'd spend it on clothes in C&A, Eve Brown's and Bus Stop. My friend Jean Greenwell worked there too. We had lots of laughs, learned how to interact with the public, and make their shopping experience a laugh too I expect. The staff were full of fun; a caring, hard working bunch of people, if a bit barmy at times! The management were great too. The lunches in the staff canteen were heavily subsidised, really tasty and great value. If other areas of the store needed extra help the Saturday girls would go and assist. Me and my pal were once called on to offer our services on the pic n mix sweetie stall. We'd been waiting ages for the opportunity, and it won't take much imagination to guess why! Suffice to say we were only asked to help on that one occasion! I didn't have a favourite sweet, I loved 'em all!

In the cafe there was a dumbwaiter (it wasn't me!). It was a small lift between the kitchen on the upper floor and the cafe, and was used for transporting crockery. One of the workers was a girl named Ann. She was a hoot, popular with staff and customers. We'd send up notes in the lift requesting fresh crockery, more gravy, or just jokey comments to the kitchen staff who we'd accuse of being on a 'go slow'. One particularly busy day we were panicking as there were no clean cups left for teas, our notes sent up to the kitchens were being ignored, until one of the kitchen staff sent a message telling us to send a girl up sharpish to help wash up. Ann volunteered and clambered into the tiny dumb waiter lift; one of the staff pressed the button and sent her on her way. I was terrified for her, and couldn't believe it would take her weight. Within seconds we heard loud squeals but luckily they were from the kitchen staff who'd got the shock of their lives when they opened the dumb waiter and saw Ann in there, ready to help, with a big grin spread across her face!

Bernadette Lane nee Crawley

My second job was during the summer holidays at Carrick's on the north corner of Gallowgate. We sold sliced and un-sliced white bread, buns and rolls, sandwiches and cakes. I was sent down to the Grainger Street premises to collect the freshly made sandwiches for the lunchtime trade. They had a machine to slice bread and another to spread butter (or margarine) on the slices before the sandwich filling was put in, this machine fascinated me. I think the fillings were egg and tomato; fish paste or cheese. In this shop as the new temporary worker, I did most of the cleaning. It was not fun keeping the linoleum floor clean on a wet day! We got a delivery of new bread and cakes at about 9.30am and all the cakes were sold by 3pm but any bread left over was sold first thing next morning. No date stamping or waste! It was our responsibility to sell the goods in the right order. Once the shelves were empty we cleaned them and the shop for the next day. I had other friends who worked for Carrick's as waitresses in their tea rooms where they got the same wage but with all the tips added on. I realised that this was a much better deal and my shop assistant career was halted until I opened my own shop in 1966. Also, at Christmas time I discovered 'working at the post office'! This was hard work but really good money.

Elspeth Rutter

TOP) MARCUS PRICE ON PERCY STREET, WITH RAY SIMPSON BEHIND THE COUNTER. RIGHT) INTERIOR OF MARCUS PRICE, 1955.

I used to be a Saturday girl at a shoe shop on Clayton Street (Timpson's I think). You got commission on sales but I was bottom of the queue so rarely had an actual customer. My job was to return loads of shoes (from the other sales people) to their boxes. I spent hours in those stacks, trying to find the right boxes. I often made mistakes, much to say I was never promoted. The toilet and staff cupboard were really manky. Many places I worked back then had filthy quarters for the staff. My daughter worked as a waitress at an elegant club by Buckingham Palace and the downstairs quarters were disgusting!

My Saturday and holiday jobs age 14 – 18 at Woolworths, Parrish's, Timpson's and Howard's gave me the incentive to study so that shop life would not be my permanent lot! I handed my pay packet over to my mother who was a single parent. Any pocket money I gave to the church for the starving children of Africa. I was about forty-two years old before I made it to Rome. When I saw the sumptuousness of the Vatican I realised what a chump I'd been. I was far too good a Catholic girl. In other words the shops of Newcastle did not benefit from my increased spending power!

Olya Bower

**TIMPSON SHOES ON GREY
GRAINGER STREET, 1959.**

In 1971 I was working in the credit office of Farnons on Nun Street. One day during my lunch hour I went to the pet shop in the Grainger Market. I've always loved animals and there was a lovely fluffy tabby kitten so I bought it, went back to work, put the kitten in the rest room where one could make teas and coffees and thought it would be alright till I finished work at 5.30pm. Later that afternoon I was summoned to the Personnel Officer's room - Miss Delaney was her name - where she informed me that the kitten had got under the floorboards and they had to get joiners in to help free the kitten. She was very annoyed and told me I was fired: I had to leave with the kitten immediately. So that was the end of that job! The kitten who I named Misty lived to be nearly twenty-three years old!

Madeleine Lydia Duployen

I left school in 1972 and my first job was in Value Stores on Shields Road on the deli counter. Lots of old age pensioners used to come in for 2oz of cheese or one slice of chopped pork! At the age of fifteen I was trusted every night to take the days takings down to the night safe further down Shields Road. Every week I had to go to the two other supermarkets on the road and find out what they were charging for sugar, bread, tea and if seen by the managers I was chased out. In 1976, when the Green Market opened I worked in McCourt's Pet Shop and let loose several budgies when trying to catch them for customers!

Sue Jeffs

I worked in Bus Stop, which was near Grey's Monument (and my dad worked in Mawson, Swan & Morgan in the book department). Bus Stop sold top fashion clothes but when I was tired I would have a nap on the shelf below the till where the paper bags used to be kept...I never got caught! I also worked in Tuxedo Junction on Market Street dressing the glass cases. I would source my stock from Handyside Arcade.

Katrina Bettaney-Kershaw

TOP) BURTON ON THE CORNER OF NORTHUMBERLAND STREET AND BLACKETT STREET, 1970. RIGHT) EVE BROWN ON NORTHUMBERLAND STREET, 1956.

My first job in the mid-70s was as a Saturday girl at British Home Stores. I was just fifteen years old and received £3.65 for the day, paid in cash. I worked in the ladies' clothing department, tidying shelves but mainly on the tills. The hours were 9am-6pm, with an hour lunch break and a fifteen minute break mid-morning and mid-afternoon. Most transactions back then were paid for in cash, or by cheque supported by cheque guarantee card. I remember scrutinising the signature on the card and worrying whether I would be brave enough to challenge a shopper whose signature failed to match. I never did challenge anyone, although sometimes people's handwriting was hard to decipher. One Saturday the department was quieter than usual but the restaurant was busy and short staffed. In a rash moment I volunteered to help out by clearing tables. I bustled around filling my tray with dirty plates and wiping the tables clean. But it transpired it wasn't just the tables that needed tidying. With a very full tray I headed off to the kitchen. Holding the tray, I wasn't watching the floor and slipped on a fallen soggy chip which I had failed to spot. The resounding crash of broken crockery brought instant silence as all turned to look at me, followed by a round of applause from a group of teenage lads I had hitherto been trying to impress. Red faced, I cleaned up the resultant mess. Strange to say, I never was asked again to help out if the restaurant was short staffed!

Babs Trevitt

I worked in British Home Stores in 1961/62; unlike modern retail shops it was all wooden counters and floors. We wore blue cotton wrap around overalls. We worked on different counters each week so you never knew from one week to the next where you would be working; but the biscuit counter was definitely my favourite. I only worked on a Saturday and for that I got £1!

Jennifer Mitchell

Working in the Newgate Street branch of the Co-op I was placed on the make-up counter, though people didn't buy a lot of make-up in those days as they didn't have the money. The working environment was different also; sleazy men were part of the territory, brushing up beside you and pushing you to get past, we put up with it though as we were only young and knew no different.

I remember one lady whose job it was to operate the lift, nothing else! She'd spend all day going up and down in the lift pressing buttons for people. I don't know how she felt but I hated my job. You worked long hours until 10pm, had only Sundays off and there were no holidays or time off: it was a different world to the annual leave entitlement, maximum working hours and flexible working arrangements of today.

At age twenty-five I worked in the chemists of the Co-op on Heaton Road. Working over Christmas we made up small boxes called coffrets which we filled with gifts such as perfume. The till didn't add up for you, it was all done in our heads and if you were short on your till at the end of the day you had to pay back the difference, so it was important to have a head for numbers. The chemist was privy to all sorts of information: women used to come in wanting something to take the baby away and during the war men used to come in wanting 'french letters'. Being a woman, men would never ask me for these, instead insisting on speaking to the chemist. In those days we were very naïve though so I didn't understand what they were asking for anyway!

Nancy Davidson

In the mid-1960s I was once six foot tall, but my elevation only lasted as long as my Cuban heeled shoes held out and by the time they had worn out, fashions had changed and they couldn't be replaced. I was only able to afford such footwear and other trendy gear (clothing) courtesy of a Saturday job at Burton's the Tailor at the bottom of Northumberland Street, just opposite what was in those days known as Cook's Corner (on the junction with New Bridge Street West). In the hierarchy of the shop I was the lowest of the low, for at that time there was a strict demarcation whereby everyone knew their place and subservience or deference was a strict requirement which the BBC comedy *Are You Being Served* accurately observed.

My job, for which I was paid fifteen shillings in cash (75p) for eight hours work, entailed recording measurements and orders taken from customers purchasing tailor made bespoke suits. In those days every adult needed and had a suit, either for work if you had a white collar job, for 'Sunday best' or, which was more likely, for weddings and funerals, and as there were no off the peg suits available a trip to a tailors was needed. There were many national and local tailors to choose from and the national chains such as Burton's, John Collier, Hepworth's and Jackson's all had branches in not only the city centre but also in the larger local shopping centres such as Shields Road, Byker.

Saturdays were very busy and long queues formed around the large table I stood at to take down the measurements, which were shouted out to me by the tailor I was working with. When the tailor (for that was what he was called even though he didn't actually make the suits) was under pressure, the time he took to measure up shortened drastically, so much so that I had difficulty keeping up with him, especially as I also had to write down the suit style details the customer required.

It was often the case that some measurements were missed; but this didn't seem of much concern, as during later quieter spells the tailor was able to make what was invariably an accurate guess as to what they should be.

TOP) BURTON ON THE CORNER OF NORTHUMBERLAND STREET AND BLACKETT STREET, 1973. RIGHT) SHOP INTERIOR, 1970S.

Customers came in all shapes and sizes, some were clearly well off and others not so much. Although I worked at the shop for only a year or two there was in that time a noticeable change in fashions, especially for the younger clientele. Customers became more adventurous in styles and cloth as they were influenced by what was happening in the so called swinging sixties and no longer were grey plain styled suits the norm. Indeed I still remember how my fellow workers were aghast at the made to measure suit that I bought (at a discounted price of course) comprising a black and white chalk pin striped single breast jacket with six inch lapels, a flared waist and fifteen inch centre vent, with matching hipster style 20in bell bottomed flared trousers without turn ups. The suit was not to their tastes, but it did match my aforementioned Cuban heels.

Joe Rogerson

I worked as a 'Saturday Girl' at Parrish's in Byker, while I was still at school back in 1977. I really loved it there, my job was in the ladies' fashion department. My manager was a lovely lady who elegantly smoked the longest cigarettes I have ever seen, she had the longest red painted nails! I thought she was the height of sophistication as she always wore seamed stockings and the highest, shiniest black court shoes! I was sometimes asked to wear and promote the teenage stock, which I really enjoyed, although the work was very varied and covered everything from creating displays, manually labelling clothes (no computers then), to hanging up clothing and jewellery. I spent a lot of time folding jumpers! Parrish's had their own 'money', which customers bought at a special rate and enabled them to save up and spend it in the store. As I was the youngest I was taken under the wing of some of the experienced staff and I learnt a lot from them. Christmas was especially exciting and

the public café was converted into a magical Santa's Grotto. The staff Christmas party was held in the function room on the top floor, the Twilight Rooms. This suite was hired out for all occasions. Sadly the store has long since closed down, but I have happy memories from those days.

Gill Clayton

It may not be common knowledge today, but both hi-fi and photography were borderline sciences right up until we approached the twenty-first century. Saturated with technical jargon that demanded translating into everyday vernacular before any of it made any sense to the average person, who perhaps only wanted a bit more creative control over their holiday snapshots, or more of a 'live concert' experience than they got from LPs on their 60s' Dansette record player. Although by vocation, occupation and pre-occupation I was, and remain, a drummer, I also had two lesser passions: namely hi-fi and photography. So, having grown up with retailers in the family, and with a head for technicalities, plus a natural disposition to advise, enlighten and educate, it was no surprise that I would look for work selling sound and vision's bells and whistles when performing music didn't butter my bread. Consequently, in 1978, having had more than enough of the vagaries and vexations of band-life – and spying a notice in the window of a new shop – I got a job selling hi-fi in a place at the top of Grainger Street (currently Starbucks).

Hi-Fi & Photomarkets occupied the ground floor and the basement, with hi-fi in the basement. A couple of years earlier, Comet had expanded its 'out-of-town' discount warehouse empire into city-centre stores: the one in Newcastle – in the Princess Square to Saville Row tunnel – was essentially a 'brown box' shop, in-as-much-as you went up to the counter and bought an item untested and un-advised. This lack of demonstration by sales advisors, along with enormous

CLOCKWISE FROM TOP LEFT. 1) THE MUCH-MISSED GEORDIE JEANS AT THEIR MONUMENT LOCATION, 1995. 2) THE TOP END OF NORTHUMBERLAND STREET, EARLY 90S. 3) LOOKING SOUTH WEST DOWN GRAINGER STREET, 1993. 4) CHRISTMAS MARKET, 2006 - NOW AN ANNUAL SHOPPING EVENT.

purchasing power, allowed for a significant drop in prices on the high street, much akin to present day Argos who were then still trading as Green Shield Stamps. It was unfortunate for the independent high-street dealer that the prices offered by Comet were simply too attractive for the majority of customers even without sales advice or service back-up. What was worse – and only to be expected, as most people are not stupid – was that customers would get all the advice they needed from a high-street trader, then go and buy the appropriate item much more cheaply from Comet.

However, our shop was different: we were a 'national franchise' with the same bulk-purchasing-power and high-profile, country-wide advertising as Comet; but with the advantage of expert sales advice. This was a concept that was new to this country: designed to survive in the emerging atypical retail market, it differed from the retail chains already in existence because each one was privately owned, and consequently unaffected by the fortunes, or misfortunes, of the other branches. And we gave Comet some stiff competition; although only in our own field, as they and Currys still monopolised discounted large appliances and TVs. Nevertheless, it was sufficient for us to establish a thriving business; and even enough to trouble the inimitable J.G. Windows, who were distinctly inconvenienced by my windows directly opposite their hi-fi department, as naturally I was given that space to display my wares.

While I mostly sold hi-fi, I was often commandeered to happily take over in the photographic department as well. All-in-all, we generated much good-will and word-of-mouth prestige, due to honest, informed advice, along with very low prices.

For a couple of years I was genuinely content. Then, in

January 1980, I was offered a gig with a band in Germany and away I went; so I'd not been that content. Unfortunately, due to eight-foot tall hoardings along the pavements of Grainger Street, while the Monument Metro station was being built, the business began to suffer and was gone as 1980 crept out. Many folk will have missed it because the independents were also disappearing, leaving a dwindling source of informed advice. Today, of course, we are all side-by-side with national franchises and, such poetic justice, Comet is now long gone – destroyed by the very thing they pioneered: because history repeats itself, and once again we buy our goods untried and unadvised by simply typing into Google. Just as a footnote: it wasn't long after our shop closed that Julian Richer opened his Newcastle branch of Richer Sounds selling TVs and hi-fi; then Frank Jessop appeared selling photographic supplies, and the status-quo was re-established.

Keith Fisher.

My first ever paid job was as a Saturday sales assistant in Littlewoods Department Store on Northumberland Street, Newcastle upon Tyne, for six weeks in the run up to Christmas during the mid-1970s. I was in sixth form, and there were at least ten other girls from my class working as Saturday assistants there. Most of my friends were on the checkouts in the Food Hall, but I was on the sweets and chocolates counter. That meant standing the whole day. My legs ached and I envied the others who were able to sit down at the checkouts manning the tills. At my counter we sold loose sweets by the quarter (four ounces - or about 110 grams or so) and if there were no customers to serve, I was expected to weigh up the more popular sweets in advance into bags of four ounces,

ready to hand over on demand when it was busy. However, quite a few customers would request two ounce bags! Coconut mushrooms and wine gums were particularly popular. We also sold bars of chocolate with flavoured cream fillings such as caramel, orange, strawberry...there were about a dozen varieties. These were extremely popular and customers would buy several bars at a time. Each bar cost eleven and a half pence each, and I got very adept at my eleven and a half times table! Customers paid at the counter, so I also had to operate an old fashioned cash register with lever buttons that you had to push down. The till did not total up for you; if a customer bought more than one item, I had to add up the cost in my head and enter the amount at the till by pushing down the appropriate buttons. However, there was a pad of scrap paper so that I could jot down the calculations if necessary. When arriving at work, once we put on our overalls (a nylon monstrosity patterned in blue check) we had to put all our personal belongings in a locker. We were not allowed to carry cash on the shop floor, and we were given tickets which we could use in the subsidised canteen. These tickets were spiked onto a safety pin which we attached to our overalls. I can still remember that we got £5.25 for the day which was a very good rate at the time; one of my friends who was working in Boots in Gosforth High Street only got £4.50 and was quite envious when she found out what I was being paid. That year, all my family got really good Christmas presents.

Grace Shaw (nee Wong)

I had a Saturday job at Amos Atkinson before leaving school at fifteen to become an apprentice shoemaker with them in 1953. The firm started business in Grey Sreet before moving to Northumberland Street where I worked. On the top floors there were six or seven men making shoes and boots and repairing riding boots, bags, suitcases; all leather goods. In a separate room on that same upper floor was where I worked with another lady. Our job was to make the uppers of the shoes and boots.

We mainly made men's shoes such as Oxfords, Derby and Brogues, the holes in which were all hand punched! I also dealt with customers that had disabilities; they would buy the readymade footwear and I would adapt them to fit their feet. Some families handed down their riding boots to other members of their family so we had to either let out the calf area of the boot or took them in, as well as patching the boots. Other work was making arch supports and metatarsal pads to fit into readymade shoes.

When I first started work we had one and a half hours for lunch so I used to catch the bus home; I lived in Walker then and of course there was not much traffic those days. I also got the bus over Byker Bridge to look at Parrish's and Beaven's on Shields Road or looked in Rowland Blaylock's on New Bridge Street. If I stayed in town during my lunch break I'd head to C&A, BHS, Littlewoods and Thomas Hunter, which was a great shop if you were a knitter, dressmaker, or any crafts like that.

Sometimes we went to Bower's for Fish and Chips, which was just off Nun Street, down a back lane towards Newgate Street; there was always a very long queue! Another popular stop was George Rye on the Bigg Market; they stocked leather of all colours and all products to do with shoe making and repairs so I often had to go there to pick up items for work.

Although I cannot recall the exact price for handmade shoes I remember they were quite expensive, hence famous customers such as Lord Ridley could afford to shop with us, he kept us very busy with his riding boots! In the 1960s we also made shoes for a lady who lived on Sark in the Channel Islands; I think her title was the Dame of Sark. Mr McNichol would have to fly to Sark to measure and fit her with her handmade shoes. Such a long way when you think; she could have had her shoes made from firms in London! Catherine Cookson was a customer in her later years; she always came with her husband and bought a few pairs of shoes at a time.

By the 1970s, we had stopped making shoes and Lobbs of London took over our customers - they would come at various times of the year to measure and fit their hand made footwear. I started working in the shop at this point but still made shoes for Mr Atkinson and his son. The names of the men's shoes we stocked were Church, Grenson, Crockett & Jones whilst the ladies brands included Bective, Renarta and Rayne, which were a brand favoured by the Royal family. Shoes for children included Clarks and Startrite.

Theresa Little

RIGHT) AMOS ATKISON ON NORTHUMBERLAND STREET, 1962. FAR RIGHT) AN ADVERT FOR AMOS ATKINSON SHOES.

There's style and service at

Amos Atkinson

THE ESQUIRE BROGUE

Uppers cut from "Martins" world renowned Scotch Gorse leather for the longest wear. The soles are made from prime long tanned bends, made by craftsman on the famous Esquire last for comfort and fit.

AMOS ATKINSON
LTD.

ESTABLISHED FOR OVER 100 YEARS

Northumberland Street, Newcastle upon Tyne

THIS BOOK IS NOW CLOSING...

Please read these final words and proceed to the checkout…

So what next for the city born to shop? Well one thing is for certain, our love of shopping won't be dying off anytime soon. Though our shopping experiences may be less market, more Primark(et) we are still flooding the city centre daily with money, or plastic, to burn. As I write, the shipping container village 'Stack' is taking shape on the corner of Pilgrim Street and is billed as being a leisure and shopping destination…though so far the businesses signed up appear to be more refreshment than retail. My crystal ball is currently at the cleaners so only time will tell whether such semi-permanent structures are the antidote in tough economic times.

Either way shopping will evolve as we do as it is part of the very fabric of our lives; it's who we are and what we do: part recreation, part keeping up with the Jones' and thankfully saves us from foraging about in bushes for food. Like it or loathe it, we all do it…so until we drop, let's shop!

THANKS

Thanks to everyone who has contributed their memories and helped shape this book. Special thanks to David Hepworth and Shawn Fairless, without whom this book would not have come to life.